Doug Simpson is a retired certified public accountant. He and his wife, Dr. Kathryn Simpson, are both avid backcountry hikers. They currently live near Waco, Texas, where they enjoy life with their children and grandchildren.

Doug is also the author of *A Walk with Buddy: The Appalachian Trail Adventure.*

To Lacey and J. Douglas

Doug Simpson

JOHN'S STORY

Perfect Love

AUSTIN MACAULEY PUBLISHERS™

LONDON * CAMBRIDGE * NEW YORK * SHARJAH

Ordering Information
Quantity sales: Special discounts are available on quantity purchases by corporations, associations, and others. For details, contact the publisher at the address below.

Publisher's Cataloging-in-Publication data
Simpson, Doug
John's Story

ISBN 9781645754220 (Paperback)
ISBN 9781645754237 (Hardback)
ISBN 9781645754244 (ePub e-book)

Library of Congress Control Number: 2021909734

www.austinmacauley.com/us

First Published (2021)
Austin Macauley Publishers LLC
40 Wall Street, 33rd Floor, Suite 3302
New York, NY 10005
USA

mail-usa@austinmacauley.com
+1 (646) 5125767

John's Story

John 1:1-14, I John 1:1-4

My name is John. I am an apostle and, along with Peter and James, part of Jesus' inner circle. Before I met Jesus, I was a fisherman. I owned a business with my brother, James. I still love the water and long for the days my brother and I worked to pull nets of fish into our boat. Now I am a fisher of men.

My father is Zebedee, and my mother is Salome. Jesus' mother Mary and my mother are sisters, so Jesus and I are first cousins. We grew up together as children and matured together as young men then adults.

This is my story of the life I shared with Jesus and the first congregation of believers. That which was from the beginning, which I have heard, which I have seen with my eyes, which I have looked at and my hands have touched— this I proclaim to you concerning the Word of Life. The Life appeared; I have seen it and testify to it, and proclaim to you the eternal Life, which was with the Father and appeared to me and the other apostles.

My narrative begins at creation. The Old Testament writers documented their creation story based on oral traditions passed down to them from generations past. People still search to explain with finite knowledge how, when, and where the universe came into existence from nothing.

Jesus and I talked about creation as we traveled the dusty roads of Judea, Galilee, and Samaria. Jesus was more than a man when our world came into being. He was deity. I like to call him the "Word of Life" because Jesus spoke God's words as he walked the ground he created. Jesus told me, "John, I started the beginning. I was with God at the start. I am the 'I AM.' All things created were created through me. Without me, nothing was created."

People can both hold tight to their truths. I believe the Word of Life. God is our Creator, and the Father and Son are one. They started creation, and together, they made our universe and everything in it. Does it really matter how "I AM" created it and when?

Jesus began his public ministry with a countenance filled with love, mercy, truth, and a spirit filled with life and light. While he was here with us, I witnessed the Son of God at the height of his earthly achievements. Jesus lived with me and the other disciples for three years. We shared everything in common with Jesus from the early days after his baptism through his death, resurrection, and ascension to the Kingdom of Heaven.

I share this story for you now to make my joy complete.

Be Prepared, the Messiah
Has Come

John 1:6-9, 14-33 Luke 1:15-17, 2:4-20, 3:1-8

Jesus lived in Nazareth of Galilee for thirty years before he began his public ministry. Many knew him as a carpenter who practiced his trade in our communities. Others knew him as a man who supported his family as the eldest son of the house of Joseph. Even more knew him as a man who spoke with knowledge in the synagogue on the Sabbath. No one knew him as God's Son.

People can speak for themselves, but their word only carries them so far. God sent another man named John to the world, to bear witness that Jesus of Nazareth is God's Son. We called this man, John the Baptist. He came from God, filled with the Holy Spirit in his mother's womb. He ministered in the wilderness to multitudes of religious people with Elijah's power and spirit.

Elijah was a powerful prophet who performed miraculous works of God. Elijah raised a person from the dead, called down fire from Heaven, and ascended to Heaven while he was alive. The Book of Malachi predicted his return before the coming of the Messiah.

Many who waited for the Messiah believed John the Baptist was Elijah incarnate and came to him to complete their baptism of repentance along the Jordan River.

I was a disciple of John the Baptist.

John the Baptist lost both his parents when he was young. He grew up with Spirit in wilderness solitude. The Word of God came to John in the fifteenth year (25-26 A.D.) of the reign of Tiberius Caesar; Pontius Pilate, governor of Judea; Herod, tetrarch of Galilee; and Annas and Caiaphas, high priests. When God spoke to John the Baptist, he began to preach in the Judea wilderness saying, "Repent, for the Kingdom of Heaven is at hand."

The people were hungry to hear God's word, and to worship and serve the coming Messiah. I marveled how fast the word of John the Baptist's powerful preaching spread. Multitudes came to him in the wilderness from Jerusalem, all Judea, and all the region around the Jordan River. The people didn't go to the temple or their synagogues when they learned the Messiah was coming soon. They amassed in the wilderness to confess their sins. John the Baptist immersed them along the Jordan River to complete their baptism of repentance.

John the Baptist was a plain-spoken man with no tolerance for the false trappings of religion in his life or the hypocrisy of religion in others. When John the Baptist saw many of the Pharisees and Sadducees, who were members of the religious elite, come to participate in the baptism of contrition he offered, he said to them, "Brood of vipers! Who warned you to flee from the wrath to come? Do not think your salvation is secure because you are a child of Abraham. Your bloodline will not deliver you to the gates of Heaven. The Messiah is close by. I baptize with water for repentance. One comes after me whose power is unlimited. He will baptize with the Holy Spirit. You still have time to repent. Make sure your baptism is sincere, so you bear fruits worthy of repentance."

These honored men stepped back when John the Baptist addressed them. They were astonished this rugged man spoke with such passion against them in front of their people. No one ever spoke to them this way. The Pharisees and Sadducees weren't convicted by his words. They were deeply angered. They heard John the Baptist, but they did not believe him. Their lifestyle and their livelihood were anchored to religious activity, not to an abiding love and awe-filled respect for the Heavenly Father. They lived by the law passed down to them to the extent they prospered and were glorified before the people in their communities.

They stood down before this preacher that day because they knew the crowd believed John the Baptist was either the Christ, Elijah, or the Prophet. These influential men turned their backs, pushed their way through the crowd, and went home. John the Baptist made an enemy that day, Jesus would face throughout his ministry.

Everyone wondered in their hearts whether John the Baptist was the Christ. The town tribunal called the Sanhedrin sent a delegation of priests and Levites from Jerusalem to question John the Baptist about his identity. I stood beside him when the delegation asked him, "Who are you?"

John the Baptist answered their questions by telling them who he was not. He said, "I am not the Christ, Elijah, or the Prophet."

When the delegation heard his response, they asked him, "Give us something to take back to the ones who sent us."

John the Baptist knew the religious leaders would intentionally cause confusion and try to obstruct the Messiah's ministry when the Christ arrived, so he answered them and said, "I am the messenger sent from God to plead with you in the wilderness. I declare to you, judge your own life and repent. Make an easy path to the Lord for the people of God who will come to embrace the Messiah."

When they heard his answer, the priests and Levites from Jerusalem asked, "If you aren't the Christ, Elijah, or the Prophet, why do you baptize with water?"

John the Baptist answered them and said, "When God sent me here, He told me to baptize with water. I tell you now, there is one who stands among you whom you do not know. I will baptize him with water, but he is mightier than me. Prepare yourself because he has come to change our world. He baptizes with the Holy Spirit."

I'll never forget the day Jesus came to John the Baptist for baptism. When John the Baptist raised Jesus from the water, I saw Heaven open to both men. They saw the Spirit of God descend and remain on Jesus, and they heard God's voice say, "This is my beloved Son, in whom I am well pleased."

John the Baptist attempted to worship the Son of God where they stood, but Jesus wouldn't allow it. Jesus lifted John the Baptist from his knees and hugged him while He shared a quiet word, then God's Son patted him on the back and disappeared into the crowd.

The next day I was walking with John the Baptist when we saw Jesus moving toward us. John the Baptist said to the people around us, "Behold! The Lamb of God who takes away the sin of the world!"

Several people heard John the Baptist make this statement and asked, "How do you know this with such certainty?"

John the Baptist paused for a moment and smiled, then he said, "God sent me to baptize with water. He told me, 'When you see the Spirit descend and remain on my Son, you will know he is the one who baptizes with the Holy

Spirit.' I tell you now, I have seen and testify that this man, Jesus of Nazareth, is the Son of God."

When John the Baptist finished speaking to us, he called Jesus to him. Then he stepped forward with Jesus and testified before the crowd who gathered around them and said, "I saw the Spirit descend from Heaven like a dove and remain upon this man. He is the Son of God. This man will change our world. The law was given through Moses. Grace and truth come through this man, Jesus Christ."

The Messiah was here. He was a carpenter from Nazareth of Galilee. He was one of our own.

John the Baptist's testimony about Jesus of Nazareth was not lost on the Sanhedrin. These men did not judge their own lives nor make a straight path to the Lord for the people who worshipped in the synagogues. They saw Christ the Lord as an adversary, not a savior. Jesus was a man with influence to overthrow their religious nation, political organization, and individual power. The religious elite threatened to remove anyone from membership in the synagogue who declared Jesus of Nazareth the Son of God. When their tolerance for Jesus expired, these men planned his death.

John the Baptist's testimony about Jesus of Nazareth was also lost on the crowds. The multitudes who came to John the Baptist, filled their lives with religious activity as they prepared for the coming Messiah. They kept up this lifestyle when the Messiah arrived and walked among them. Did these people shift their devotion to the Son of God at any point in Jesus' ministry? The multitudes came to Jesus at different times to see him perform mighty miracles and speak like no other man, but few openly believed in his name. They feared their leaders and loved their worldly lifestyle more than they loved or respected the living God.

God did not leave us when Jesus ascended to Heaven. He left us his Spirit to follow and find comfort on the Day of Pentecost. The Messiah is here, today.

Where does our devotion rest? Do we share a common life with Jesus Christ as we follow the Spirit of Life in our daily lives? Or do we live to satisfy other people's expectations as we set aside a spirit life and follow another person's wants and hopes?

Come and See

John 1:35-51

The next day Andrew and I stood with John the Baptist at Bethany on the other side of the Jordan River. Andrew was also John the Baptist's disciple. We watched the crowds pass before us at the marketplace while we listened to John the Baptist reflect on his ministry. He dedicated his life to announce the arrival of the Messiah to the people, and the Messiah was finally in our midst. He told us, "My ministry will come to an end as the Messiah's ministry begins. You have both been good and faithful disciples, but it is time for you to leave me and follow Jesus of Nazareth."

When John the Baptist saw Jesus walking through the crowd, he pointed him out to us and said, "Behold the Lamb of God!" We turned to the Baptist and we all smiled. John the Baptist gave us both a hug, then looked us in the eyes and said, "Go. Follow him. It is his time."

Thereafter, Andrew and I left John the Baptist and followed Jesus through the crowd.

Jesus eventually turned around and asked me, "John, what do you seek?"

We were both caught off guard. What did we seek? Andrew and I sought the Messiah. How did we respond to the Son of God?

We said, "Teacher, where are you staying?"

Jesus smiled and said, "Come and see." We both came and saw where he stayed and remained with Jesus for the rest of that day.

Andrew slipped out to find his brother Simon later and said to him, "We have found the Messiah!" Simon saw his brother's countenance and accepted his word. Simon also sought the Messiah. He left their fishing boat and joined Andrew and me at Jesus' dwelling.

The next day Jesus left for Galilee while we put our affairs together. Jesus found Philip in Bethsaida and said to him, "Follow Me." Philip walked away from his life to go after Jesus.

When he had the chance, Philip found his friend Nathaniel in Cana and said to him, "We have discovered the person whom Moses and the Prophets wrote. He's Jesus of Nazareth, the son of Joseph."

Nathaniel looked surprised and said, "Philip, are you certain? Can anything good come out of Nazareth?"

Philip smiled at his friend, put his arm around his friend's shoulders, and said, "Come meet Jesus and decide for yourself."

Jesus greeted Nathaniel like an old friend when he approached. Nathaniel had never seen Jesus before, so he asked, "How do you know me?"

Jesus looked into Nathaniel's eyes with a reassuring countenance and said, "Nathaniel, I saw you sitting under your fig tree long before Philip called on you." Nathaniel's spirit, like all of us who banded together with Jesus, was overcome with joy.

He answered Jesus and said, "I have waited a long time for you, Rabbi. You are the Son of God. You are the King of Israel!"

Jesus smiled and said, "You speak well, Nathaniel."

Then Jesus stood up and said to all of us: "Nathaniel, you believe in me because I told you I saw you under the fig tree. You will see greater things than this. Before we finish our work together, you shall see the heavens open and angels shall ascend and descend upon the Son of Man."

Can you imagine Jesus' character and leadership qualities? Jesus' disciples were ordinary people like us. The disciples did not know Jesus before they met, but Jesus knew them. When Jesus came to each disciple, they set aside their ways, and followed him without hesitation. Their spirits filled with joy and their lives changed forever.

God knows our heart and mind long before we sense his Spirit come to us. He will come in love with open arms to embrace us; just as we are, not as we hope to be. Come and see. Your life will change forever.

First Miracle

John 2:1-11

Mary was Jesus' mother. She raised her son to be a man of integrity—a person respected by their community.

On the third day we were together, a family friend from Cana was married. Jesus, Mary, and all the disciples were invited guests to the wedding festivities. The reception was a joyous affair. As the celebration progressed, the master of the feast ran out of wine.

Mary knew the Godly power her son possessed before Jesus began his public ministry. I saw Mary turn to her son and heard her say, "Son, the bridegroom has run out of wine to share with the guests. Jesus, we can help our friends."

Jesus looked at his mom and said, "Mother, why do you bring this problem to me. I didn't bring extra wine."

Mary smiled and hugged her son. When she stepped back, Mary stared into her son's eyes with a knowing look and said, "Jesus, if you choose, I know you can provide more wine for this marriage celebration."

Jesus put his arm around his mother and said, "Yes Mother, I can, but it's not time to reveal my powers to the world."

I was surprised when Mary smiled at her son, nodded her head, and then turned to the servants and said, "Whatever he says to you, do it."

The Son of Man responded favorably to his mother's request. We watched Jesus discretely turn the water delivered by the servants into wine without drawing attention to himself. The bridegroom was blessed, and the festivities continued when a delicious wine was made available to all the guests.

We were all in a new environment. Jesus was our leader. He had a plan for the day, and he had a schedule for his ministry. We enjoyed the day as we watched Jesus closely to learn more about him. When Jesus granted Mary's request, our faith in him solidified. He revealed his power to perform miraculous signs to us and we believed in him.

As evening came, Jesus extended all our blessings to the bride and groom as we gathered to leave. When we were outside the courtyard, he said to us, "I must leave you now to prepare for my Father's work. I will be gone for a time. Pray for me because the task is hard. Use this time to get your affairs in order. When I come back for you, your lives will change forever."

We believed Jesus' words and we placed our faith in him. We hugged him, then we walked to our homes to wait while Jesus left for the Jordan River.

We live busy days focused on meeting the demands of hectic schedules. How do we respond when Spirit prompts us to accept challenges that force us outside our normal routine? Do we offer a good excuse and turn our back? Most do. We can also listen to Spirit's voice and follow his lead with a servant's heart.

God is honored when we quietly act without thought of recognition. We may never know who is watching us, and we may never understand how our actions impact another person's life. The joy comes in the act, not the recognition. It is always interesting to see how time and resources are restored when we follow Spirit's lead.

Temptation

Matt 4:1-11, Luke 4:1-13, DT 8:1-5, James 1:2-4

Jesus left his disciples in Cana and returned to where he was baptized in the Jordan River. Jesus only had the clothes on his back when God's Spirit led him from the river into the desert to live by himself. No one was present to encourage, distract, display affection, or lend a helping hand.

God humbled Jesus in the wasteland to test his heart, and see whether Jesus would obey God's commandments under duress. The Lord allowed Satan to test Jesus in this isolated place where the nights were cold and the days were hot. Food was lacking to satisfy his hunger and water was scarce to quench his thirst. Satan tormented Jesus physically, mentally, and emotionally in this solitary world for forty days.

Sometime during the forty days, Jesus hit the marathon runner's physical and emotional wall. His spirit remained steadfast throughout this cruel ordeal, but his body and mind weakened dramatically.

On the fortieth day, Satan saw his opportunity to take Jesus for his own. Satan came to the Son of God when Jesus suffered with severe dehydration and starvation. Satan challenged Jesus and said, "Why do you hunger, Jesus? If you are the Son of God, you have the power to turn these stones into bread. Why suffer when you can eat to your satisfaction?"

Jesus answered Satan with a swollen tongue through cracked lips and said, "My Father placed me in this desert for a reason. It's not my place to question my Father. My powers shall only be used for His purpose. He will provide for my every need in His time. Satan, you know man does not live by bread alone, but on every word that comes from the mouth of God."

Jesus was exhausted when he finished speaking. The devil smiled when his adversary leaned back against a boulder to rest. He took this opportunity to sweep Jesus from the desert and take him to the temple in Jerusalem. They stood together at the building's highest point and stared across the holy city. Satan looked into Jesus' eyes and said, "How do you know you are God's Son?"

Jesus returned Satan's gaze and said, "Satan, you know the Father and I are one."

The devil shook his head 'no,' and said, "Prove it. Throw yourself from this building. If you are the Son of God, your Father will command His angels to protect you from harm."

Jesus calmly answered Satan and said, "You know I am God's Son. It is written, 'Do not put the Lord your God to the test.'"

When the devil heard Jesus' response, Satan took him to a remarkably high mountain and showed him all the kingdoms of the world. Their brilliance was appealing to the eyes. Satan placed a hand on Jesus' back and said, "I will give you all this, if you will bow down and worship me."

Jesus burst out laughing when he heard the devil's proposition. He answered Satan and said, "You know that I am 'I AM.' My kingdom is in Heaven. One day soon, you will bow down and worship me. Now get behind me, Satan. For it is written, 'Worship the Lord your God, and serve Him only.'"

When Satan finished tempting Jesus, he left God's Son in the desert to return at a more opportune time.

Jesus walked into the wasteland filled with the Holy Spirit. He was a private man who had lived a full life as a carpenter for thirty years. He clung to the Spirit in him for strength and companionship as he endured Satan and the elements for forty days. When the devil departed, angels came to Jesus and carefully restored his health.

Jesus was prepared for public ministry when he walked out of the desert. He and the Father were one.

Jesus did not question God when he suffered in the desert or was tempted by Satan. And he did not allow his circumstance to defeat him when he was weak and alone. He accepted what he must endure and clung to the Holy Spirit in him for love, strength, and companionship.

When he walked from the wasteland, Jesus was prepared to serve the Father all the way to the cross.

Trials are worthy opponents that can undermine faith. God allows us to face adversity as He tests us, as Satan tempts us, or as life experience simply brings hardship our way. We will persevere to the perfect end if we remain content with God in our circumstance. If we accept what we must endure and cling to the Holy Spirit to sustain us with His love, strength, and companionship, then God will prepare us through adversity to change our world.

When trials finish their work, we will either be mature and complete, lacking in nothing; or we will be broken, walking alone in darkness. Strive for the higher choice in the Holy Spirit's protective illumination.

Jesus Sets the Tone of
His Ministry

John 2:12-22, Matt 14:1-5, Matt 4:12-25

Jesus left the desert and walked to Bethany on the other side of the Jordan River. When he arrived, he could see John the Baptist's disciples approaching. Their countenance was filled with concern bordering on fear. Jesus embraced them when they came to him. He asked, "What has happened? Where is John the Baptist?"

They said, "Herod has arrested him. The soldiers bound John the Baptist and put him in prison."

Jesus was disturbed by this news. He did not expect the Roman government to act against their ministry. He asked the disciples, "Do you know why they arrested him?"

The men shook their heads 'yes,' then the spokesman said, "John the Baptist told Herod he could not have Herodias, his brother Philip's wife, for himself. He's still alive because Herod believes he's a prophet."

Jesus pondered this information for a moment, then he told the disciples, "John the Baptist needs you. Go to him and serve any way you can. Tell him the ministry he proclaimed about me begins now in Galilee."

Jesus left Bethany and walked to Nazareth to visit with his family and gather fresh belongings. When he walked through his home's front door, his mother was shocked at the weight he lost. She hugged and kissed her son, then moved to the kitchen to prepare Jesus' favorite meal.

The family gathered around the kitchen table Joseph made for Mary, while she cooked. Jesus described his wilderness ordeal with his mother and brothers as they ate. When they finished their meal and the kitchen was clean, Jesus revealed to his family he was the Messiah.

They talked together late into the night. When everyone went to their bed, Mary's heart was sad. The brothers did not believe Jesus' story.

Jesus rose early in the morning to leave Nazareth. He came into the kitchen and saw his mother making his breakfast. She smiled at her son and said, "Good morning, sweet boy! Drop your bag by the door and come sit while I finish cooking your food."

Jesus dropped his bag as she requested, then he happily hugged his mother before he took his place at the kitchen table.

Mary turned away from the stove and said to Jesus, "I am disappointed in your brothers."

Jesus said, "Don't be, Mom. Today they think of me with their mind and feel with their heart. They will come to me when they listen to Spirit. Do not despair. My brothers will minister with God's Spirit to their world in this lifetime."

Mary smiled through tears that stained her cheeks, then she said, "I trust your words, Son."

Mary pulled up a chair and sat beside Jesus after she served his breakfast. She touched her son's arm and asked, "What are your plans, Son?"

Jesus smiled between bites and said with excitement in his voice, "I begin my Father's ministry today. I will live in Capernaum. When I get there, I will start to gather my disciples, then preach throughout Galilee. We'll stay in Galilee until we go to Jerusalem for the Passover Feast."

When the sun began its morning ascent, Mary watched her son walk away from their home with his bag over his shoulder. She smiled through tears of joy as she remembered the words the Lord said through the prophet: "The virgin will be with child and will give birth to a son, and they will call him Immanuel—which means, God with us."

Capernaum is located next to the Sea of Galilee. James Peter, Andrew, and I ran our fishing operations from this lake with our fathers.

Andrew and Peter were casting their nets into the lake when Jesus walked up to them on the shoreline and shouted, "Peter and Andrew, it's time. Come, follow me, and I will make you fishers of men!"

The brothers gathered their fishing nets and hurried to greet Jesus. He helped them secure the nets in their boat. After they put on their outer garments, they took Jesus down the shoreline to the spot they knew James and I were fishing with our father.

We were in our boat preparing our nets to fish when Jesus arrived. I turned the boat around and came to shore as soon as I saw Jesus.

That day, we all abandoned our fathers, our businesses—everything we valued before we met Jesus. We left it all behind and followed him.

We traveled together throughout Galilee. Jesus taught in the synagogues on the Sabbath and in the open air during the week. He preached the good news that God's Kingdom was near, and he healed every disease and sickness the people presented.

News of his powerful gifts quickly spread throughout Galilee. People brought him all who were sick with various diseases, those suffering severe pain, seizures, paralysis, and the demon-possessed. He healed them all.

Large crowds from Galilee, the Decapolis, Jerusalem, Judea, and the region across the Jordan River followed Jesus to witness these miraculous signs. We saw God's power manifest itself through him.

When it was almost time for the Passover Feast, we walked with Jesus to Jerusalem to worship at the temple. When we entered the temple courtyard, the sound and smell of livestock and the noise of moneychangers overwhelmed us. We came for the religious experience and walked into a carnival atmosphere. This holy place of worship had changed into a marketplace where oxen, sheep, and doves were sold, and money was exchanged.

Jesus was outraged. What had happened to God's house? We had never seen Jesus irate. He was truly angry with the religious guardians responsible for maintaining this holy place and the marketers earning a profit. Jesus raged against these godless people who turned this uncommon place—a holy place where people were supposed to meet their revered God—into a worldly place where evil rejected God.

Jesus set the tone for his public ministry when he entered the temple courtyard. He confronted religious sin and the religious elite head-on with his voice. He demanded God's house be returned to a holy place of worship. He gathered rope, made a whip of cords, and unleashed his fury on the marketplace. He overturned tables, spilled coins across the temple floor, then drove the livestock and birds from the temple shouting, "Take these things away! How dare you make me Father's house a market."

The people were stunned, but no one laid a hand on Jesus to stop him.

When Jesus cleared the temple, I watched the religious elite move from the courtyard shadows to challenge Jesus. They didn't defend their actions. They didn't apologize for their behavior and turn to God. And they didn't arrest Jesus. They knew he was right. They spoke with stiff necks and hardened hearts and said, "What sign do you show us to prove your authority to do all this?"

Jesus did not teach, preach, or perform a miracle to justify his actions to these hardened men. He responded with this riddle and walked away, "Destroy this temple, and I will raise it again in three days."

Jesus spoke to me later in plain language about this confrontation. He said, "John, I wasn't talking about a building made of stone. My Father has told me how my earthly ministry will end. I spoke to those men about my death and resurrection. Remember this promise when you grieve on the darkest day: they will kill me, but death can't hold me. You will see me again. I will rise from the dead to live in three days."

God does not pour affliction upon us as divine retribution for our sins. We do this to ourselves by the way we choose to live life without God. Our problems do not start at the end of this life. They begin when we stop listening to our spirit and turn away from God to live our own way.

Lives can turn upside down when people separate from God. They lose sight of their purpose. We know anyone born of God does not continue to live life separated from God.

The consequence of living apart from God can be a heavy burden for a person to carry. The weight manifests itself in harmful emotions, dangerous habits, destructive behavior, or disease that destroys people, relationships, families, careers, organizations, and communities.

God still loves us despite our behavior or attitude. He does not leave us. We leave Him. He still pursues us with open arms, ready to eliminate this burden and restore His children to a new life.

If we come home, God will take away the sting our mistakes create and bring about a time of refreshment to anyone who changes their ways, embraces God's love and mercy for their life, and holds on to a common life with Jesus Christ through the Holy Spirit.

Our Father loves us. He holds us tight in His grasp to nurture and protect us. He will pursue us when we set Him aside to focus on the rituals and activities we sponsor.

Jesus fought for the temple's sanctity. The Holy Spirit will fight to bring us home when we make mistakes and lose our bearings.

Human Eyes and Understanding

John 2:23-25, Acts 3:19-20

Jesus performed numerous miracles while he ministered to the people who attended the Passover Feast in Jerusalem. God and Jesus were one standing before the multitudes. The crowds marveled at Jesus' gifts as they watched him. Many observed what he did and believed in his name because his physical talents and intellect were great.

Jesus came to them as the Son of God, but he did not commit himself to them when they professed to believe in his name. Jesus knew their hearts and minds. They believed in him because he peaked their intellectual and emotional curiosity. They embraced Jesus with human eyes and understanding. Jesus did not coddle, manipulate, or compromise himself to gather a congregation this way.

The people saw Jesus as a mighty man instead of the Son of God, so Jesus rejected the crowd's praise and walked away.

The Heavenly Father is not an idol. He is "I AM." We cannot construct God in our image and guide Him with our own idea of who He is and what we want in time of need. Jesus rejected this mindset at the Passover Feast in Jerusalem.

God is not a man and He is not an object. God is Spirit. He knows our hearts and minds and seeks a spiritual relationship with those who will worship Him in spirit and truth. God rejects those who follow Him with human eyes and understanding. Our Father is faithful to those who live life in His perfect love, who expect to hear His voice and see His hand in their daily activities.

Born Again in Spirit

John 3:1-21

We finished supper with Jesus and sat around the fire enjoying the night sky when Nicodemus stepped from the shadows into our light. Nicodemus was a Pharisee and the "Teacher of Israel." Jesus recognized him as a man he saw in the temple courtyard. Nicodemus was present when Jesus performed miracles to demonstrate he spoke for his Father through his teachings.

Jesus invited the Teacher of Israel to join us. Nicodemus accepted the offer and said to Jesus, "We know you are a teacher come from God. No one can do these signs unless God is with them. I am a Jewish scholar. I have studied Jewish history and the law my entire adult life. After listening to you teach and preach, I am convinced I may be full of knowledge about God and law, but I do not have a personal relationship with God. Please tell me what I must do to see the Kingdom of God."

Jesus saw the scholar was sincere, so he answered him, saying, "Nicodemus, God delivers us to the world in the flesh as body and soul. We can spend our entire life in a natural state as we seek to satisfy the desires of our flesh while our spirit lies dormant. Nicodemus, everything in the natural world—the cravings of sinful people, the lust of our eyes, and the boastful pride of life—it all comes from the world, not from God.

"God is Spirit. He seeks those who will worship Him in spirit and truth. If the path to Heaven is built on a person's religious activity and thoughtful consideration without a spiritual relationship with God, then Nicodemus, you are a model for all to follow. You are an elite religious leader who carries the title, 'Teacher of Israel.' You've obtained a scholar's knowledge about God and religion through your life's work, but Nicodemus, you do not know God personally. You must be born of Spirit to live in the Light of Life, to see the Kingdom of God, and to experience eternal life. You will live alone to your own end in your natural state without Spirit in your life, no matter how robust your knowledge may be and how faithful you are to your religious belief.

"Nicodemus, based on your question to me tonight, you realize a person will not enter Heaven just because they are born to a certain bloodline. The same is true for people who make a personal decision to live a religious lifestyle based on their own belief, or they perform a religious act, like baptism or church membership, to please another person. You must be born again into a spiritual state through God's Spirit to become a child of God and enter the Kingdom of God."

Nicodemus listened carefully to Jesus, then answered him and said, "How can this be? Jesus, as you can see, I am an old man. How can I be born again when I am old? Can I enter my mother's womb a second time?"

Jesus shook his head and smiled, then answered, "No Nicodemus, I refer to Spirit. Your body is your body as your spirit is your spirit. You cannot enter the Kingdom of God unless your spirit is born again through God's Spirit."

Jesus paused for a moment and stared toward each man sitting beside the fire with the eyes of a loving teacher. When he spoke, we listened closely as he said to Nicodemus, "I am the Light and Life sent by God. I came from Heaven to provide God's children a clear path to righteousness and contentment in all matters.

"The life I give is eternal. Anyone who believes in me will be born again of Spirit when I send the Holy Spirit to live with them and in them. God is their Father and they will be His child. My Father's children live in fellowship with God through me and they shall not perish but have everlasting life.

"Nicodemus, God did not send me here to condemn your world, but to save those who hold onto the life and light I offer. Those who believe me will embrace me, follow me, and do what is true with God. God's children will live in the open, so their deeds are seen clearly. Those who do not believe in me do not wait for my condemnation. They are already condemned.

"Nicodemus, those men you work with denounce me because their deeds are evil. Evil hates me and stays away from the open. Those men live and practice in the shadows of religion, so their evil deeds are not understood by the people they lead."

The night turned quiet as we considered the truth Jesus spoke. Jesus eventually stood and walked to Nicodemus. Jesus helped him to his feet and embraced him, then said, "Nicodemus, you have much to consider in this life if you want to see the Kingdom of Heaven."

The Son of God did not come from Heaven to condemn an old religion. And he did not come here to start a new religion full of rituals and activities. He came to give life and initiate a spiritual relationship with God's children by sharing a common life with them through the Holy Spirit.

Spirit and Truth

John 4:1-42

Before Herod arrested John the Baptist and placed him in prison, John preached and baptized in the land of Judea. After Jesus finished his work at the Passover Feast in Jerusalem, we came to the same region to teach and baptize.

We drew the Pharisees' attention as our ministry quickly surpassed John the Baptist's. Jesus was concerned when he found out the Pharisees knew he baptized more disciples than John the Baptist. He decided it was best for us to leave Judea.

The next morning, we headed toward Galilee passing through Samaria. Around the sixth hour, we reached a city called Sychar. Jacob's well was close by so Jesus stopped to rest at the well while we went into town to get food for everyone.

A Samaritan woman came to the well to draw water for her household. As was the custom, the woman ignored Jesus and began her work. Jesus was the one who broke the silence. He said to her, "Please give me a drink."

The woman was surprised when Jesus spoke. She looked at him and said, "Why do you talk to me and ask for a drink? You are a Jew, and I am a Samaritan woman. Sir, Jews have no dealings with Samaritans."

Jesus shook his head as if he agreed with the woman, then answered her and said, "If you knew me and you knew the gift of God I want to give you, you could ask me, and I would give you living water."

The woman laughed for a moment then smiled at Jesus and said, "Well Sir, where do you get this water? This well is deep, and you have nothing to draw with. Are you greater than our father Jacob who gave us this well?"

Jesus rose to his feet and looked directly at the woman. He said, "You focus on your thirst. I am offering you a spiritual gift. Anyone who drinks water from this well will thirst again. But whoever drinks from the water I give will never thirst. The water I give transforms in a person into a fountain of water springing up into everlasting life."

Jesus was talking to the woman about the Holy Spirit. Spirit life begins with a taste and transforms in a person to a fountain of spiritual gifts and understanding.

The woman heard Jesus speak but did not understand his words. She said, "Please give me the water that I may never thirst or come back to this well to draw for water."

Jesus said, "Go get your husband and come back."

The woman said, "I have no husband."

Jesus said, "You are right to say you have no husband. You have had five husbands and the man you live with now is not your husband."

The woman dropped her head in shame when she realized Jesus knew her secrets. She stayed quiet until she felt God's grace and mercy flow from Jesus to her.

She looked at Jesus with a renewed spirit as she said, "Sir, I can tell you are a prophet. Our fathers worshiped on this mountain. You Jews tell us we must worship at the temple in Jerusalem to receive salvation. Where should I go to worship the living God?"

Jesus answered her and said, "The time has come to stop worshiping the Father on this mountain or in Jerusalem. God is Spirit. He is seeking true worshipers who will worship Him in spirit and truth where they stand."

The woman was surprised by the prophet's answer. She lowered her eyes, ran her hand across the lip of Jacob's Well then responded to Jesus with a note of skepticism, saying, "I know the Messiah is coming. When he comes, he will tell us all things."

When she finished speaking, Jesus paused for a moment, then touched her hand and said, "I am the Messiah."

At this point we came back, and marveled that Jesus was talking to a woman in public. However, no one said, "Why are you talking with her?" Then the woman left her watering pot and went into the city.

She sought out the men and said, "Come see a man who told me everything I ever did. He knew my secrets. Could he be the Christ?"

The people left the town and came to Jesus. Many of the Samaritans believed in him because of the woman's words. Many more believed because of Jesus' own words. We stayed with the Samaritans for two days.

When we left, the people said to the woman, "Now we believe, not just because of what you said but because we have heard Jesus and we know he is the Christ, the Savior of the world."

We live in a world filled with unspoken bias. We suppress our prejudice to educate our children and conduct business and commerce but feel most comfortable sharing life with those we know.

God loves His creation and those who live in His world. His Light shines across every nation, race, skin color, creed, gender, age, economic status, and background. We cut short the rich life God plans for us when we set boundaries that limit our life experience to those who share our way of life. God's love has no limitations, and the Holy Spirit has no boundaries.

Why don't we live life participating in kind moments, sharing gifts and time with those who live outside our favored world? Why is this? We have so much to learn from each other.

This is a way we know God lives in us and with us: we live like Jesus lived. Jesus judges no one. People condemn themselves when they walk away from the Holy Spirit's gift of life. Jesus shared himself with a person who was considered an outcast by many people's standards at the time. She was a Samaritan woman who was divorced from five husbands and who was now living with a man outside marriage.

This kind moment Jesus shared with her resulted in changed lives for an entire community.

Your Son Lives

John 4:43-54

We left the Samaritans after two days and returned to Jesus' home country of Galilee. The Galileans were glad to see Jesus again. His neighbors, friends, associates, and acquaintances all saw Jesus as a mighty man of great talent and wisdom. They enjoyed watching the miraculous signs he performed at the Passover Feast.

However, Jesus had walked away from these people in Jerusalem because of their unbelief. He knew his home country rejected his message by the time we reached Cana, the city where Jesus turned water into wine.

While Jesus experienced disappointment in his home country, a nobleman in Capernaum heard Jesus had returned from Judea to Galilee. He was greatly relieved because his son was extremely sick. He left his servants in charge of his child and walked from Capernaum to Cana to ask Jesus for help.

When he arrived in Cana, he forced his way through the crowd of unbelievers to reach Jesus. Above the noise of the crowd he said, "Rabbi, my son is near death. I know you can heal him. Please come to my home and heal my child before he dies."

I watched Jesus place his hand on the nobleman's shoulder and walk him away from the crowd. When they were in a quieter place, Jesus encouraged the man and said, "Go home. Your son lives."

The nobleman believed Jesus' word and started home. As the man walked the road to Capernaum, he met his servants who gave him the great news, "Your son lives! His fever left him yesterday at the seventh hour."

The father grinned a smile that spread across his face as he remembered it was the seventh hour Jesus said to him, "Your son lives."

As tears of joy streamed down his cheeks, he said aloud for all to hear, "Thank you, Jesus. You truly are the Messiah; the Son of God."

This was the second miraculous sign Jesus performed, having come from Judea to Galilee. Jesus shut down His healing ministry in Galilee because the people had stubborn minds and hardened hearts.

What counts with God is the faith and awe-filled respect we bring before our Heavenly Father.

Broken Laws

John 5:1-15

After Jesus' time in Galilee, we returned to Jerusalem to attend another religious feast. Jerusalem had a large public pool called Bethesda. There was a popular belief surrounding the pool. The legend was, an angel came to Bethesda and stirred the water. Many people believed that the first person to enter the pool after the angel stirred would be healed of their infirmity. The structure had five porches. A multitude of sick, blind, lame, and paralyzed people lay on the porches each day waiting for their opportunity to be healed.

We walked with Jesus to Bethesda on the Sabbath to heal a person with God's power. Jesus planned to create a teaching moment with the religious elite before the congregation at the temple courts. A man laid by the pool who suffered with his infirmity for thirty-eight years. Jesus saw him on the crowded porch and came to his side and said, "Do you want to be made well?"

The man answered Jesus and said, "I come to Bethesda often, but I have no one to put me in the pool when the water stirs."

Jesus looked at the man with compassion and understanding, then bent down and placed his hand on the man's shoulder and said, "Stand up, take up your mat and walk." The man was immediately healed. When he stood and turned in his excitement to thank Jesus, he discovered Jesus had disappeared into the crowd.

As the healed man passed through the crowd rejoicing in his good fortune, a group of religious men confronted him and said, "Today is the Sabbath. It's against our law for you to carry your bedding."

The man looked at these men in disbelief and said, "This is the first time I have walked in thirty-eight years. The man who healed me told me, 'Take up your mat and walk.' Can't you be happy for me?"

The religious men stared at the man with contempt then asked him with hardened hearts, "Who is the man who told you to pick up your mat and walk?"

The one who was formerly lame did not know who healed him because Jesus withdrew into the crowd. The religious men threatened to throw the man out of the synagogue if he did not come to them at once if he spoke to Jesus again. When they finished intimidating the healed man, the religious men sent him on his way.

Jesus found the man in the temple later that day, and said to him, "You look great. Stop sinning now or something worse may happen to you."

The man was confused where his loyalty should lie. On one hand, Jesus had healed him. But on the other hand, the religious men had threatened him. After Jesus left, the man decided to reveal the name of Jesus of Nazareth to the religious men.

The religious elite stole the lame man's joy for a time. They struck fear in him with their threats. The healed man had a choice: he could focus on the menacing remarks and suffer with anxiety or worse, or he could face the religious men with meekness, and rejoice in his new life when he stood on his feet and walked.

We may face bullies like the religious leaders in our life. They try to intimidate us by exerting their power over us. If we focus on the harm an intimidator can cause to our circle of life, we may compromise our beliefs and stumble down an emotional black hole. This is a lonely time.

Jesus says, "I am the way, the truth and the life." If we concentrate on God's Spirit and rely on His strength for our strength during dark times, blessings will reveal themselves to mitigate our predicament. Hold onto these gifts and the Holy Spirit will equip us to find contentment in our hardship. We may not experience moments of euphoria, joy, or happiness when we focus on the Holy Spirit, but we will be more than satisfied with God's perfect love wherever we stand.

Remember, God holds us in His hand and our Father will not let us go. The peace, security, confidence, and understanding we need to face our intimidator will come forth in the strength and integrity that God gives us in every situation—good, hard, or mundane.

Bear Witness of Me

John 5:16-47

The religious elite hunted Jesus down in the temple as soon as the healed man gave them his name. When they found us in the crowd, they tried to bully Jesus. Then they sought to kill him because he healed a cripple on the Sabbath.

Jesus stood up to them and said, "My Father always works, even on the Sabbath. I work when my Father works."

The crowd murmured to each other, "The carpenter from Nazareth just said God was his Father."

Yes, Jesus plainly told the crowd He was equal with God. The religious elites were outraged by this proclamation. Their anger turned to hatred, and they carried murder in their hearts. John the Baptist's testimony about Jesus meant nothing to them. The religious elite wanted Jesus dead.

Jesus knew what they thought and felt, yet these men did not intimidate Jesus. He stood before them and the crowd and answered them all saying, "Truthfully, I can't do anything on my own. I watch my Father and do what He does. God heals on the Sabbath and so shall I.

"I understand why you could doubt me. I have lived among you for thirty years. Yes, some of you know me as a carpenter. Some of you know me as a man who teaches in the synagogue. Others know me as the eldest son of Joseph in Nazareth. If I were speaking on my own behalf, I would deserve this public outrage.

"But there are other witnesses. You all heard John the Baptist give expert and reliable testimony about me. Even greater than John the Baptist's witness is the testimony you have seen in the very works the Father has given me to complete. The miracles show the Father is with me and you have missed it! You do not hear His voice because you aren't listening, and you do not see Him testify about me in the scripture as the path to salvation because you aren't looking. The scripture speaks all about me, yet you are unwilling to accept from me the life you say you want."

Who bears witness that God is in us and the collective church, today? No one, if we live a life void of God's Spirit in our daily life. We may use the name Christian, but we simply bear witness of ourselves. We have no credibility to represent God within our circle of life. Without the Spirit, our words are founded on human understanding, and our witness to those around us is false. Our godly activities have no capacity for belief before our children, our grandchildren, our spouse, our friends, and our co-workers. As we've seen in this lifetime, Christian churches are emptying because next generations do not see evidence of a relevant God in our collective life.

This is a way we know God's Spirit lives in us and with us: God's children live like Jesus lived. Jesus' countenance was filled with love, mercy, and truth; and his spirit was filled with life and light.

People who are full of faith and the Holy Spirit live in the open where their deeds are clearly seen to have been accomplished through the Holy Spirit. God's children love the Lord with all their heart, soul, and mind; and they love their neighbors as themselves.

God completes His perfect love in the world through His children's love for their circle of life. When we obey God's command to love our neighbors as ourselves, our Father's love is reflected through us. Since the Day of Pentecost, the Holy Spirit is the one who bears witness for us and the collective church.

Jesus' words to Nicodemus at their fireside chat in Jerusalem should weigh heavy on our world today. He said, "No matter how robust our knowledge may be and how faithful we are to our religious belief, we will live alone to our own end in our natural state without Spirit in our life.

"A person is foolish to believe they can enter Heaven because they are born to a certain bloodline. The same is true for people who make a personal choice to live a religious lifestyle based on their own belief, or they perform a religious act to please another person. A person must be born again into a spiritual life through God's Spirit to become a child of God and enter the Kingdom of God. Our body is our body, and our spirit is our spirit. We can enter God's Kingdom and experience His abundant life as our spirit is born again through God' Spirit."

Jesus did not come here to start a new religion. Jesus came to initiate a spiritual relationship with those who wish to live with him and seek to worship the Father in spirit and truth. Our Father bared witness for Jesus as he completed his work. Just like Him, the Son of God bears witness for us as we live our life in the open where our deeds are clearly seen to have been accomplished through the Holy Spirit.

Five Loaves and
Two Small Fish

John 6:1-15

When the feast finished, we crossed to the far shore of the Sea of Galilee. A great multitude came after us because they saw all the miraculous signs Jesus performed in Jerusalem. We needed time to regroup and rest, so we climbed a mountain to separate from the crowd. Jesus watched the people gather as we talked among ourselves.

Jesus asked Philip, "Where can we buy bread to feed all these people?"

Philip looked in his purse to count our money and said, "Lord, we have two hundred silver pieces. Two hundred silver pieces worth of bread isn't enough to feed this crowd crumbs."

Jesus smiled at Philip and said, "Philip, I didn't ask you how we are going to pay for food to feed this crowd, I asked you where we need to go to get the food."

My friend Andrew was listening to the conversation. He pointed to a boy in the crowd and said, "Lord, I see a boy over there with five barley loaves and two small fish, but that will barely feed a small family."

Jesus patted Andrew on the back and said to the rest of us, "You count and plan with what you have at hand. I measure by the abundance yet to be seen. Stand up now and invite the crowd to sit down for a meal."

We organized the crowd because we believed in the one who provides what we cannot see. When we finished seating the multitude, we counted five thousand families. The boy gladly gave Jesus his fish and bread. Jesus gave thanks to God for the meal and began to distribute the bread and fish to the disciples who then shared with the multitude. When everyone was finished eating, there were twelve baskets with leftovers.

The disciples walked down the mountainside in the light and life of Jesus. Each man understood his task, and they gave Jesus their resources. Jesus didn't ask them to feed 5,000 families with two hundred silver pieces worth of bread or five loaves and seven small fish. He asked them to organize the crowd. Jesus provided the bread and fish and they simply followed his command to serve the food. When Jesus and His disciples finished, the crowd's hunger was satisfied, the food provided was more than enough, and the disciples' faith in Jesus grew stronger.

The people marveled how God was at work through Jesus. They said to each other, "This must be the Prophet who is to come."

Jesus heard their words and knew their thoughts. The people wanted to force him to be their king. They sought him because he had the power to satisfy their physical hunger.

Jesus did not hesitate. He turned his back on these people in disappointment and he returned to the mountain by himself.

Jesus said, "You count and plan with what you have at hand. I measure by the abundance yet to be seen." When everyone was finished eating, there were twelve baskets with leftovers.

We usually walk with him into the unknown to address challenges that surpass our known gifts, resources, and understanding. These situations are troubling when we face them by ourselves. This is a reason God asks us to follow his Spirit to complete his work.

The 5,000 families would not have eaten an evening meal if they depended on the disciples. We set up for failure when we move away from Spirit to address a challenge with our own understanding; or worse, we never even start because we believe we are insufficient. Be patient.

We count and plan with what we have at hand. God measures by the abundance yet to be seen. When God calls us to a task, focus on the task, and the One who gives will provide in ways we can only imagine.

Stormy Waters

John 6:16-21

When evening came, we left Jesus on the mountain to pray while we got in a boat and began to cross the sea toward Capernaum. When the sun set and dark night arrived, heavy winds caused the sea to roil in deep turmoil. Each man in the boat prayed to God to save our lives.

After we rowed in stormy waters in pitch black night for several miles, we saw an apparition walking toward us on the water. We were terrified as the figure approached our boat, but the spirit shouted to us in a familiar voice and said, "It is I; do not be afraid." We heard Jesus' voice over the wind and sea, and gratefully received our savior into the boat. When Jesus settled in, we immediately arrived at Capernaum.

Light is not seen in light. Light illuminates darkness. Those who walk with Spirit see God clearly as they navigate the difficult periods of life.

The disciples followed Jesus' instructions to row without him to Capernaum and found themselves battling a treacherous storm. Jesus placed their lives in jeopardy when he sent them on their way without him. Who did the disciples think would save them when the sea engulfed them? They fought for their life as they prayed for calm water on a pitch-black night. The last thing they expected to see through driving rain and rolling sea was a figure walking toward them on water. Imagine their fear. They were terrified when the answer to their prayers appeared in the distance. They didn't recognize Jesus at first, but they knew his voice and they gratefully let him into the boat.

God does not always answer our prayers as we might expect. He answers our prayers His way, at His time, with His resources. The disciples prayed God would stop the storm to calm the sea. After all, no man walks miles across water in deep turmoil to calm a stormy sea—except Jesus. When we call God's name, we should wait for His response with open eyes and a curious heart. Expect the unexpected or we may miss the answer to our prayers.

These Words Are Hard

John 6:22-66, Luke 22:14-20

The next day, people from the crowd of five thousand searched for Jesus on both sides of the Sea of Galilee. They found him teaching at the synagogue in Capernaum. They interrupted Jesus' sermon and asked him, "Rabbi, when did you get here?"

Jesus answered them and said, "I came here last night. I left you on the other side by the mountain because you seek a king. You did not come here today because you saw my Father at work through me. You are here because I fed you bread, and you were filled.

"It's a mistake to labor in this lifetime for things that perish. Work hard for the gifts the Son of Man gives. They endure to everlasting life. It is the Spirit who gives life; the flesh profits nothing. It's important you remember this: the words that I speak to you are Spirit, and they are Life."

When they heard these words, they asked Jesus, "We want to do God's work. What is God's work?"

Jesus answered them and said, "This is the work of God: believe in the one He sent from Heaven. I am the Son of God. Believe in me."

The crowd pressed closer to Jesus when he spoke words claiming his deity and asked, "What works will you do that we may see it and believe in you? Our fathers ate bread from Heaven every day they walked in the desert."

Jesus pressed his hands together in front of his face as if to pray, then he said to the people, "Is that why you are here? Do you want me to feed you every day? Stop focusing on your physical hunger. Moses did not feed your fathers in the wilderness. My Father sent food from Heaven every day to satisfy His children's hunger and those people did not live to see eternal life. They died in the wilderness. Moses did not feed you yesterday. My Father sent living bread from Heaven to feed your spirit and you focused on the nourishment my disciples provided to satisfy your physical hunger.

"Listen to me. God is Spirit. The time has come when my Father seeks true worshipers who worship Him in spirit and truth, not people who perform sacrificial rituals based on the rules of religious law in Jerusalem. If you want food that lasts, feed your spirit by believing in me. Think of me as living bread and water sent from Heaven by my Father to feed your spirit. My Spirit is the bread and water that nourishes the soul and leads you to everlasting life."

The religious people in the crowd asked Jesus for a sign so they might believe his words. The Son of God stopped and thought about the words and actions he would share with his disciples at their last supper together. With this thought fresh in His mind, Jesus spoke to the crowd and said, "Remember, my Spirit is the bread and water that nourishes the soul and leads you to everlasting life. You seek a never-ending supply of bread to eat. I tell you, whoever feeds on my flesh and drinks my blood shares in a common life with me."

Many disciples began to complain when Jesus made this statement. They said, "These are hard words. Who can understand what Jesus says?"

Jesus knew his disciples were grumbling among themselves. He turned his attention from the remnant of the five thousand people still in the synagogue and to all his disciples and said, "Do my words offend you? I told you, the words I speak are about Spirit, and they are life. Religion focuses on a person's physical relationship with their God. 'I AM' is Spirit and love. My Father did not send me to you to start a new religion, but to show you a new life, walking with God in spirit and love.

"But some of you still do not believe. I am the Bread of Life. He who comes to me shall never hunger spiritually, and he who believes in me shall never thirst spiritually. You have seen me, and yet you do not believe. No one can come to me unless it is granted to him by the Father."

God's Spirit illuminated their thinking, but the people still did not understand Jesus of Nazareth. From that time many of his disciples went back to their previous life and walked with Jesus no more. When the crowd vacated the synagogue that morning, only twelve disciples stood with Jesus. He looked around the empty room and said to us, "Don't you want to leave me?"

Peter did not hesitate to answer the question. He stepped forward and spoke for our small group. He put his arm around Jesus' shoulder and said, "Lord, where else can we go? You have the words of eternal life; and we believe you are the Christ, the Son of the living God."

These are hard words. Do Jesus' words still offend people? Most walk away from all religion when their spirit convinces them to leave their natural lifestyle and actively share life with the Son of God through the Holy Spirit.

Some bond with people of like mind in religion's shadow life and continue to live a worldly lifestyle without "I AM." They claim the name of God, but their life is not a witness of the living God. They bear witness of themselves and lead fruitless lives until they die.

What can we say to "I AM"? Peter said it best for us, "Lord, we believe. Where else can we go? We want what you offer. You have the words of eternal life."

My Father's Time

John 7:1-13

Jesus' ministry caused an uproar in Jerusalem, so he chose to walk with us in Galilee rather than return to Judea when we left Capernaum. The religious elite hated Jesus and gave orders to kill him because he threatened their way of life.

Some people in Jerusalem praised Jesus and others complained about him in private conversation. Some said, "He is good."

Others said, "It's quite the opposite. He deceives the people."

No one spoke openly about Jesus because everyone feared what the religious leaders might do to them.

Jesus' brothers still did not believe Jesus was the Christ, the Son of the living God. Surprisingly, they were not aware his life was in danger.

When the Feast of the Tabernacle was at hand, they encouraged their brother to depart Galilee and return to Jerusalem with them. They said to Jesus, "If you want to be a public figure you need to stop hiding and go where the world can see you. If you want to perform signs, let the disciples you lost at Capernaum see you perform the miracles in Jerusalem that you perform here."

Jesus broke off a piece from the loaf of bread he was eating and passed the bread to his brothers. When they finished eating their shares, Jesus said to them, "My brothers, you are good men, and I love you, but you do not understand. The Jerusalem world hates me because I testify that its works are evil. The religious leaders plan to arrest me and have me killed while I attend the Feast of the Tabernacle. You can leave for Jerusalem now because no one hates you. I will follow when my Father's time is right for me to attend."

The brothers were always confused when Jesus spoke to them this way. When they gathered their belongings and went up to the feast, Jesus followed behind, attending the feast in secret.

Jesus' life was hard. He was misunderstood and condemned instead of appreciated when he followed God's Spirit to complete his Fathers work. Evil did not fear God or respect the Son of God when Jesus lived with the disciples.

How can we expect people to fear God or respect us now? Jesus didn't own the Pharisees' response to him, and we don't own our world's response to us when we live in and with the Holy Spirit.

How can we live in an environment filled with difficult situations? Like Jesus, we don't race to confrontation. Jesus patiently waited on the Lord. He stayed quiet as he actively listened for the Lord's voice. When the Father prompted, Jesus allowed the gifts of the Holy Spirit to work through him.

God's command for us is very simple: Speak God's truth in the open as we love our neighbor as ourselves. And when we are wronged, be quick to forgive.

Yes, You Know Me

John 7:14-30

Jesus entered the temple courts to teach despite the threats to his life. The Feast of the Tabernacle was half over as the crowd gathered to hear him speak. The Levites and priests in the crowd were amazed by Jesus' knowledge of doctrine. They asked aloud, "Isn't this man the carpenter from Nazareth of Galilee? He's never studied with us at the temple. How can he possess this knowledge?"

Jesus turned to these men and said, "My Father in Heaven gave me these principles. This is not my doctrine, but His who sent me."

Jesus stopped teaching then and spoke plainly to the religious elite who gathered around him. He said, "Why do you seek to kill me?"

When Jesus confronted the religious leaders with this accusation, they hid behind the voices in the crowd who said, "You must have a demon. Who wants to kill you?"

Jesus ignored the people's response and focused his attention on the Levites and priests. He said to them, "You are astonished I healed a man on the Sabbath. Doesn't Moses' law require circumcision, and you circumcise males on the Sabbath? What is the difference between minor surgery and a major healing? How can you be angry with me because I completely heal a man on the Sabbath? Be merciful and use your common sense. Do not judge based on appearance. Judge according to moral excellence and goodness."

The religious elite had no response for Jesus, but some of the people in the crowd from Jerusalem did have a thought. They said, "Isn't this the one they seek to kill? Have the rulers changed their mind? He speaks boldly, and they say nothing to him. How can this be? Do they truly believe he is the Christ? We know this man. He is a carpenter from Nazareth of Galilee."

When Jesus heard the people, he cried out and said, "Yes, you know me, and you know my hometown, but I did not come here by myself. You do not know me because you do not know the One who sent me to you. I know Him, for I am from Him."

When Jesus declared His deity again, the crowd in the temple courtyard burst into chaos. The religious leaders tried to take him then, but no one could lay a hand on Jesus because his hour had not come.

I like to believe Jesus was surrounded by legions of angels who protected him at that moment. How often do we judge a person based on appearance or another person's account of the person? The world missed the Son of God in their midst because they judged Jesus based on who he was instead of who he is.

People in the crowd spoke that day and said, "This man came from Nazareth. We know him." The statement was not true, but it sounded good, and it led many people astray.

Those who walk with Spirit in love assess situations and people in goodness with an open heart and mind. Like Jesus, we don't view our world in black and white. We recognize life is a spectrum of gray as we show mercy and grace and use common sense to engage others with God's understanding.

They Called the Temple Guard

John 7:31-53

We returned to the temple court the next day and Jesus taught without fear. Many people who listened to him believed he was the Son of God. As they pressed against each other to get closer to Jesus, they spoke among themselves and whispered, "When the Christ comes, will he do more signs than this man has done?"

The Pharisees heard the crowd murmur these words and returned to the chief priests to report their concerns. The Pharisees shared what they experienced, and they all agreed Jesus had to be stopped while his influence could still be controlled.

The chief priests called in the temple guard and ordered the officers to arrest Jesus. These men were not afraid to destroy the life and ministry of the one sent by God.

The last day was the greatest day of the feast. On this day Jesus stood before a large crowd and cried out, "If anyone thirsts, come to me and drink. He who believes in me, as the scripture has said, 'out of his heart will flow rivers of living water.'"

When Jesus finished speaking that afternoon, many who heard him said, "Surely, this man is the Prophet." Others said, "This is the Christ."

Some of them wanted to take Jesus, but no one laid hands on him. The temple guard officers were moved by the power in Jesus' words and eventually returned to the chief priests and Pharisees empty-handed. The chief priests asked the officers why they didn't take Jesus.

The officers answered honestly and said, "No man speaks like this man."

The Pharisees were beside themselves when they heard the officers respond to their question. They said, "Are you also deceived?" The officers stood in silence, keeping their personal belief to themselves.

Jesus risked his life when he returned to the temple. Still he came and he taught without fear. Jesus did not compromise his integrity. He spoke God's truth with the power in him. He was one man, but he did not come alone. God was with him and many believed in him.

He saw the temple guard dressed in military array. Jesus knew the soldiers were in attendance to arrest him. He felt the Pharisees' hatred. He knew the Sanhedrin was prepared to kill him, yet Jesus spoke like no man had ever spoken to those people. When he finished speaking, He walked away from the temple on his own terms.

Confrontation is a part of life we can't always avoid. There isn't a set answer for how God's children behave when we confront adversaries. On one hand, Jesus was outraged when he saw the temple had changed from a holy place of worship into a marketplace where oxen, sheep, and doves were sold, and where money was exchanged on the temple court floor.

Devotion to God's House consumed the Son of God. He was very angry with the religious guardians responsible for maintaining this holy place and the marketers earning a profit. Jesus raged against the godless people who turned this uncommon place—a holy place where people were supposed to meet their revered God—into a worldly place where Dark had rejected the Light.

On the other hand, when his life was at risk, his countenance was filled with mercy and truth. His spirit was filled with life and love, and he spoke God's words like no man had ever spoken to those people.

I believe Jesus showed different emotions because he faced different adversaries. He confronted evil when he displayed his anger in the temple courtyard. He showed mercy and love when he faced innocent people whose souls were lost in their religion. God's children know the difference as we walk with Spirit in love and view our world with God's understanding.

We can cause irrevocable harm when we push Spirit to the side and engage in emotional brawls. We are at our best when we address people with Spirit's understanding. When we are confronted, it's best to remind ourselves at the beginning, we do not own the adversary's response.

The wise person stands firm with integrity and loves the unlovable from the overflow of God's perfect love. The Holy Spirit will be reflected through us as we speak truth in the open with meekness, confidence, and respect.

Go and Sin No More

John 8:1-11, John 1:16-17

The day ended, and everyone went to their home, except Jesus. Jesus retired for the night at the Mount of Olives. Early the next morning Jesus returned to the temple. All the people gathered around him in the courtyard, so Jesus sat down and began to teach.

Before long a group of scribes and Pharisees entered the courtyard and created a ruckus at the outer edge of the crowd. As they moved through the people toward Jesus they shouted, "Teacher, we have a question for you."

When they had everyone's attention, the men presented a frightened woman to Jesus and said, "Teacher, we caught this woman in the very act of adultery. We believe Moses law commands us to stone her. What do you say?"

The woman cringed with fear as she waited for Jesus' response. Her life depended on this man's answer. If this teacher followed the law, she was about to suffer a painful death for a thoughtless indiscretion.

She was surprised when Jesus ignored the question and stooped to the ground and began to write with His finger. *Perhaps He didn't hear the question,* she thought to herself. As she watched Jesus write, she realized he was documenting names and sins in the sandy dirt.

The scribes and Pharisees repeatedly asked Jesus their question until he finally raised up. Jesus stared at each accuser with the solemn look of a stern judge, then pointed to the ground by his feet, and said, "Whoever among you is without sin, you be the first to throw a stone at this woman."

After he offered this challenge, he squatted back down and continued to write. The religious men recognized the secret sins attached to their names. One by one, beginning with the eldest, these hard-hearted men left with shame through the crowded courtyard before Jesus exposed their sin to the public.

Jesus stood again when the last accuser left the courtyard. He looked across the crowd then asked the woman, "Where are those accusers of yours? Has no one condemned you?"

The woman raised her eyes and spoke to Jesus with a trembling voice. She said, "No one has condemned me, Lord."

Jesus shook his head in agreement, then reached down and took the woman's hands into his own and said, "Neither do I condemn you. Go and sin no more."

The crowd was moved by Jesus' wisdom and compassion. Several were present the day John the Baptist testified concerning Jesus. His words became the crowd's reality watching Jesus address the woman and her religious accusers.

John the Baptist said, "From the fullness of his grace we have all received one blessing after another. For the law was given through Moses; mercy and truth come through Jesus Christ."

Many carry secret sins from the past we hope never become public. We still carry guilt and shame from this time which impacts our ability to live a clean life. We all fall short of our hopes at different times in our life.

God does not condemn us. Why do we condemn ourselves or each other? Why not release the hatred, guilt, and shame attached to these mistakes before these emotions overwhelm all that is good in us? Seek the help that is needed to lay these harmful emotions at Jesus' feet for his disposal, then go and sin no more.

Who Am I

John 8:12-59, Ex 3:13-14, Rev 1:8, Rev 22:13, John 14:6

Jesus wiped the dust from his hands against his outer garment, as his sandaled feet smoothed the ground that contained his writings. When he finished, the crowd settled, and Jesus began to teach again. He spoke to the people and said, "I am the Light of the world. He who follows me shall not walk in darkness but have the Light of Life."

Jesus started to expound on this important spiritual truth when another group of Pharisees stood up before the crowd to interrupt Jesus' teaching. They said, "You bear witness of yourself. What you are telling these people is a lie."

The crowd leaned toward Jesus when the Pharisees started their argument. They all heard the rumor the chief priests planned to arrest Jesus and have him killed. They were surprised when Jesus lowered his eyes for a moment, then slowly shook his head before he rose to his feet to face his accusers.

Jesus lifted his eyes toward Heaven, then cast a sad smile toward these men before he began to speak. When he spoke, he said, "We have discussed this before. You either don't listen or you don't care about the truth. You judge according to what you see. I judge no one. If I judge, my judgement is true because I am not alone. I am with my Father who sent me. It is written in your law that the testimony of two men is true. I am one who bears witness of myself, and the Father who sent me bears witness of me."

Jesus' accusers looked around the courtyard with open arms and asked sarcastically, "Where is your Father?"

Jesus answered the religious accusers and said, "You do not know me or my Father. If you knew me, you would know my Father."

No one attempted to seize Jesus when he finished speaking these words. The Pharisees weren't through with Jesus. They asked him, "We know who you are Jesus of Nazareth, son of Joseph. Who do you say you are?"

Jesus cast the same sad smile toward these men, then said, "Nothing has changed. I am who I said I am since the beginning. You are from below. I am from above. You are from this world. I am not of this world. You will die in your sin if you do not believe I am who I claim to be. You will indeed die in your sin. When you kill the Son of Man, you will know I am who I claim to be, and I do nothing on my own but speak just what the Father has taught me."

Jesus was aware many in the crowd put their faith in him while he spoke before his accusers. He turned away from the religious men then and shared his love with the believers in the crowd. He walked about, touching shoulders, shaking hands, and returning encouraging smiles before he began to speak again.

Jesus said, "If you hold firm to my teaching, you really are a disciple of mine. And you shall know the truth and the truth shall make you free as you live with me in the Light of Life."

The Pharisees interrupted Jesus then and said, "We are Abraham's descendants. We are slaves to no one. How can you say, 'You will be made free?'"

Jesus took his time to measure his words and scan the crowd before he said, "Sir, you misspeak. I refer to darkness and sin. People sin in darkness and remain separated from God. Anyone who sins is a slave to sin. A slave does not have a permanent place in a family, but a son has a permanent place forever. Therefore, if the Son of God makes you free from the bondage of sin to enter the Kingdom of Heaven and on to eternal life, you are free indeed.

"I know you are Abraham's descendants, but you seek to kill me because my words do not fit into your lifestyle. I speak what I have seen with my Father. You do what you have seen with your father. You say Abraham is your father. If you were Abraham's children, you would do the works of Abraham. Instead, you seek to kill me because I told you the truth which I heard from God. Abraham is not your father. You do the deeds of your father. You say God is your father. If God were your father, you would love me. You do not love me because you do not know me and you do not understand me because you are not able to listen to my words. You do not believe me because I tell you the truth. He who belongs to God hears God's words. You do not hear because you do not belong to my Father. Your father is the devil."

The religious accusers lost their composure at this point and shouted a degrading comment at Jesus. They said, "You are a Samaritan and have a demon."

Jesus shook his head and smiled, then said to the crowd, "I do not have a demon. I honor my Father and these men dishonor me. I do not seek glory; but my Father seeks awe-filled respect from you. I tell you the truth, if anyone keeps my word, they shall never see death."

The Pharisees were elated with their adversary's response. In their minds, they finally trapped Jesus with his own words. They said, "Now we know you have a demon. Abraham and the prophets are dead, and you say, 'If anyone keeps my word, he shall never taste death.' Are you greater than Abraham and the prophets who are dead? Who do you make yourself out to be?"

Jesus answered them and said, "Your father Abraham rejoiced to see my day, and he saw it and was glad." The religious elite were completely taken back by Jesus' response.

They said to him, "You are not yet fifty years old, and you are going to tell us you have seen Abraham. Who are you?"

Jesus stood before the religious accusers and the believers in the courtyard and answered the Pharisees' question, saying, "Who am I? I tell you the truth, before Abraham was born, I was 'I AM.'"

The Pharisees got the answer they wanted from Jesus. Jesus declared He was the God of the Israelites. At this declaration, the religious elite picked up stones to throw at him. Jesus escaped the madness by hiding himself, then walked through their midst to leave the temple grounds.

Moses spoke to God at the burning bush while he tended the flock of Jethro, his father-in-law. Moses said, "Suppose I go to the Israelites in Egypt and say to them, 'The God of your fathers has sent me to you,' and the people ask your name. What shall I tell them? God said to Moses, I AM WHO I AM. You tell the Israelites; 'I AM' has sent you. This is my name forever, the name I am to be remembered from generation to generation."

"Who am I, you ask?" Jesus answered their question this way: "I tell you the truth, I AM Who I AM."

Moses met "I AM" by a burning bush, and his encounter with God radically changed his life forever. The religious people encountered "I AM" again on the temple grounds and they tried to stone him.

How can this be? Somewhere along the way, these people became distracted with daily life and their hearts hardened. The people stopped loving God as He loved them. Then they left God behind to live a worldly lifestyle as they lost touch with their spirit. They didn't recognize "I AM" when he stood before them. They listened to their religious leaders and judged Jesus from a worldly perspective.

God still loved these people so much He freely gifted eternal life to them by setting aside His Son's life as a sacrifice for their sins. And how did these people respond to His gift? They concluded Jesus was merely a mighty man from Nazareth and tried to kill him with rocks. How can a world be so lost in itself?

No One Sinned

John 9:1-41

As we passed through the temple gates and entered the Jerusalem streets, we saw a blind man begging for coins. I came up beside Jesus while we walked and asked, "Lord, why has this man been blind since birth? Did his parents sin or did he sin?"

Jesus shook his head 'no' and said, "No one sinned. Good people experience adversity. God's most cherished works are revealed through the trials we face in our life."

As Jesus walked toward the blind man, we reminded Jesus, saying, "Lord, today is the Sabbath. Is today a good day to heal?" Jesus answered us as He continued to move toward the blind man.

He said, "I must do the works of my Father during the day. The night is coming when no one can work. If I am in the world, I will bring glory to my Father and expose this dark world for what it is; a hollow place separated from God."

Having said this, Jesus came to the blind man and embraced him with the healing power manifest in him, then he spit on the ground and made a paste of clay. Jesus anointed the man's eyes, then told him to wash himself at the pool of Siloam. When he returned to us, the blind man could see.

When his neighbors and others saw the blind man, they marveled at the miracle and took the man to the Pharisees to give an account of what happened. When the man finished telling his story, the Pharisees were divided. Some made the argument Jesus was a fraud because he didn't keep the Sabbath. Others said a sinner could not perform such a miraculous sign. They finally agreed the man was probably never blind and called for the parents to testify.

The parents feared their leaders. The Jewish leadership had decided if anyone confessed that Jesus was the Christ, they would be put out of the synagogue. The Pharisees asked them, saying, "Is this your son, who you say was born blind? How does he now see?"

The parents answered and said, "He is our son and he has been blind from birth. How he sees now, we do not know. You will have to ask him. He is of age. Ask him."

So, the Pharisees called back the blind man and said, "Give God the glory! We know Jesus is a sinner."

The healed man answered them and said, "I don't know if he is a sinner. I do know this. I was once blind and now I see."

The Pharisees hurled insults at him and said, "You are his disciple. We are Moses' disciple. We know God spoke to Moses. We do not know where Jesus is from."

The man who was formerly blind shook his head and said, "You are amazing. Jesus opened my eyes and you do not know where he is from. No one has ever opened the eyes of someone blind from birth. If this man was not from God, he could do nothing."

The Pharisees chastised the man and said, "You were born in sin and you are teaching us?" And they cast him out of the synagogue. The blind man lost his place of worship but gained his sight when he encountered Jesus.

Jesus sought out the healed man when he heard he'd been cast out of the synagogue. When he found him, he said to him, "Do you believe in the Son of God?"

The man answered Jesus and said, "Lord, tell me who he is that I may believe."

Jesus placed his hands on the man's shoulders and looked him in the eyes, then said, "You have seen him, and you are talking to him."

Then the man said, "Lord, I believe!" And he worshiped Jesus.

God's children are not protected from hard circumstances. Living a Spirit-filled life does not mean we are happy, joyful, or euphoric at every turn of events. We can suffer tragedy, disappointment, sadness, and depression, especially when we carry grief's heaviest burden. We live through the full emotional spectrum for a reason—we are alive.

In our lowest moments, we may search for someone to blame for our misfortune. When we can't find fault in another person, we often blame ourselves. Some blame God. The truth is, no one may be at fault.

If we don't forgive; we may never make peace with ourselves. If we aren't careful, we can carry forward unresolved pain and anger that snuffs out our ability to rest in the Spirit's love and grace.

God's most cherished works are often revealed through the trials in our lifetime. Let the Holy Spirit honor us through adversity with the full knowledge we are in our Father's grasp and He will not let us go. We will begin to heal when we forgive without condition and seek shelter in the Spirit's perfect love and grace.

The Good Shepherd

John 1:9-13, 10:1-21

We walked from the temple to the outskirts of Jerusalem with a crowd that included a group of Pharisees. Jesus stopped to share a story with us when we passed a shepherd and his hired hand. These men were gathering their flock of sheep from a pen.

Jesus said, "I tell you the truth, the watchman opens the sheep pen door for the shepherd. The hired hand follows the shepherd through the door. Anyone who enters the enclosure another way is a thief. Watch the sheep. The shepherd calls the sheep by name, and they come to him in the sheep pen because they know his voice. When the shepherd finishes gathering his flock, the sheep will follow him through the door into the fields to graze because they know him and trust him."

Jesus and the Pharisees watched the shepherd and his hired hand gather his sheep. When they left the pen, Jesus stepped from the crowd and called to the sheep by name. The sheep did not turn their head toward Jesus because they did not recognize his voice.

As the flock passed by, Jesus waved to the shepherd and the hired hand, then turned back to the Pharisees and said, "The good shepherd gives his life for the sheep, but a hired hand is not the shepherd. He does not own the flock and he will not sacrifice himself for them because he is not invested in the sheep. He is simply earning a wage. When the hired hand sees a wolf coming, he will leave the sheep and run while the wolf catches the sheep and scatters them. The good shepherd will fight the wolf to his death, protecting the flock.

"I am the good shepherd. I know my sheep, and my sheep know me."

Jesus used this practical application to describe the life he came to gift to the world, but the Pharisees did not understand how his story applied to them. Therefore, Jesus said, "This is the truth. My Father is the watchman and I am the gate. I am the entrance to God's unending love and salvation. Believers receive God's love through me; a perfect love that begins as a spark in a person's spirit and grows into the flame of eternal life through the Holy Spirit.

"I am also the good shepherd. I know my sheep and my sheep know me. I will give my life for the sheep. Sheep are my Father's children. They know my voice and follow my illumination in this dark world. When I call their name, they come to me and follow my voice as they live with Spirit in abundance.

"The hired hand is anyone who attempts to lead others in godly ways with their own understanding. When trouble comes, the hired hand flees, and the people who follow the hired hand scatter in darkness. Satan is the thief. The thief tries to sway unbelievers to kill, steal, and destroy the life and love I give to my Father's children. The sheep do not leave my protection to follow the thief; in fact, they run from the thief because they do not recognize the stranger's voice."

Jesus paused for a moment and everyone watched as the flock mixed with the people who crowded the street. When we lost sight of the shepherd and his sheep, Jesus talked about His life and death with the Pharisees. He said, "I am the good shepherd. You are the hired hand. I know my Father's children and my Father's children know me, just as my Father knows me and I know my Father. I set aside my life freely with love so God's children may escape death and live their life in abundance until they pass from here on to the Kingdom of Heaven and eternal life. My Father loves me because I will lay down my life that I may live again."

We walked away with Jesus when the Pharisees began to argue over his words. Some said, "Why do you listen to him? He has a demon and he is mad."

Others responded back and said, "These are not the words of one spoken by a demon. Can a demon open the eyes of a blind man?" When they turned to question Jesus, we had already crossed over the hill and were gone from their sight.

Everyone is born in the flesh with body and soul. The Son of God gives understanding to everyone coming into the world through our spirit. There comes a day when the Father opens every person's spirit to His Son, through God's Spirit. Everyone recognizes the true Spirit that comes to them for a time, and for others, many times.

Most people reject God when He comes to them. They choose their worldly lifestyle and remain in darkness to death. Some receive God. He gives them the right to become children of God as their spirit is born again in God's Spirit.

The Spirit knows us, and the believer knows the Spirit. Like the good shepherd and his sheep, when He speaks to us, we recognize His voice, and follow Him as He guides us away from a life without Him to an abundant life overflowing with the Holy Spirit.

God's Spirit protects us in our world. The tempters no longer rule our life because God's Spirit lives in us and with us. When evil comes to take us back, God fights for us.

Solomon's Porch

John 10:22-42

Winter arrived, and we returned to Jerusalem to celebrate the Feast of Dedication. We entered the temple with Jesus and began to walk along Solomon's Porch when Jesus was surrounded by Pharisees who said to him, "How long will you keep us in suspense? If you are the Christ, tell us plainly."

The circle closed tight as Jesus took time to take in each man's face. He recognized several who walked with him when he shared the good shepherd story. This crowd was not here to engage in spiritual debate. Jesus knew they came to seize him and take him before the chief priests to be killed.

Jesus was not intimidated. He slowly moved around the circle and began to speak in a strong voice, saying, "I have told you many times who I am, and you do not believe. All the signs and miracles I do in my Father's name bear witness of me, but you still do not believe because you are not my sheep. My sheep hear my voice. I know them, and they follow me. I give them eternal life and they shall never perish. You think you have power over me, but you don't. No one shall snatch my sheep from my hand. My Father, who gave them to me, is greater than all, and no one can snatch them from His hand."

When he finished speaking these important words for all believers, he spoke the words the Pharisees came to hear. Jesus answered them and said, "My Father and I are one."

The Pharisees roared with rage as they picked up stones again to kill Jesus with rocks. The Son of God stood his ground before the mob without fear. He raised his voice and said, "You have seen me do many great miracles through my Father's healing power. For which good work do you stone me now?"

The mob answered him and said, "We aren't stoning you for your good works. You are going to be killed because of your blasphemy. You make yourself out to be God."

Jesus answered them and said, "I understand. Do not listen to my words. If I do not do the works of my Father, don't believe. If I do, believe the works that you may know that the Father is in me and I am in Him."

The Pharisees heard enough. The circle collapsed on Jesus, but he escaped their grasp.

We left Jerusalem with Jesus and went to the place beyond the Jordan River where John the Baptist first baptized, and there we stayed. Many people came to Jesus and said, "John the Baptist did not perform signs, but his words about this man are true." Many believed in Jesus there.

This is God's promise to His children, "If you hold firm to my teaching, you really are a disciple of mine. And you shall know the truth and the truth shall make you free as you live with me in the Spirit of life."

We shall never perish. God knows us, and we follow Him from death to life and on to eternal life. The dark world thinks it has power over Jesus Christ, but it doesn't. Have faith and believe this: Our Father is greater than all, and no one can snatch us from His hand.

Remove the Stone

John 11:1-54

While we ministered with Jesus beyond the Jordan River, he received word that Lazarus, a very close friend, was sick at his home in Bethany. Jesus brought us together when he heard the news, and said, "Lazarus is sick. His sickness will not lead to his death, so let's wait to visit him."

Two days later, Jesus gathered us together and said, "Let's go to Judea. It's time to visit Lazarus and his sisters, Mary and Martha." We were surprised when we heard Jesus was ready to return to Judea.

We said to him, "Rabbi, Is this a good idea? The Jews just tried to kill you in Jerusalem. Bethany is only two miles from the temple. The Pharisees will track you down and seize you this time."

Jesus smiled. Then, with the resolve of a warrior preparing for battle, said, "Our friend sleeps. I go to wake him."

We relaxed for a moment and said, "This is good news. We can stay here, Lord. If Lazarus sleeps, his sisters will nurse him back to good health. He will get well on his own."

Jesus shook his head no, then he spoke plainly, "Lazarus is dead. Even if he is dead, let us go to him. The infirmity came to him for God's glory that the Son of God may be glorified. I am glad I wasn't there so you may believe in my power over death."

Despite the confidence in his words, we were sure Jesus would die at the hands of the Jews in Bethany. Thomas said to us, "Let's go with Jesus that we may die with him." So, we came to the outskirts of Bethany and stopped.

When Martha heard Jesus was coming, she left her home to meet him. When she saw Jesus, she broke down in his arms and said, "My brother has been in the tomb four days. If you had been here, my brother would not have died. Even now, I know whatever you ask God, he will give you."

Jesus held Martha close as she wept and said to her, "Martha, your brother will rise again."

Martha nodded her head and said to Jesus through her tears, "I know he will rise again in the resurrection at the last day."

Jesus stepped back then and held Martha's hands in his own. He smiled at her through his own tears and said to her, "Martha, I am the resurrection and the life. He who believes in me, though he may die, he shall live. And whoever lives and believes in me shall never die. Do you believe this?"

Martha gave Jesus a quizzical look and said, "Yes, Lord. I believe that you are the Christ, the Son of God, who is to come into the world."

Jesus put His arm around Martha's shoulder then and said plainly, "Martha, Lazarus died but he shall live again. If you believe, you shall see the glory of God through your brother's death. Now wipe away your tears and send Mary to me."

Martha went back to the house where the religious people from Jerusalem were comforting her sister. She secretly called Mary, saying, "The Teacher has come, and he is calling for you." As soon as Mary heard Jesus was nearby, she rose quickly and went to him. The religious people thought she was going to the tomb to weep, so they followed her to the place where Jesus waited.

When Mary saw Jesus, she fell at his feet and said to him, "Lord, if you had been here, my brother would not have died."

The religious people saw Jesus comfort Mary and said, "If this man can open the eyes of the blind, he could surely have kept Lazarus from dying."

Jesus saw Mary weep and the religious people who were with her cry. He groaned in the Spirit, deeply troubled by the heavy burden of pain they displayed in their grief.

Jesus wept. He comforted Mary while she wept.

When she stopped sobbing, he helped her to her feet and said, "Mary, my Father will be glorified through Lazarus' death. Please take me to the tomb now."

Jesus still groaned inside when they came to the tomb. The tomb was a cave with a stone laying against the opening. Jesus called out, "Remove the stone."

Martha said, "Lord, are you sure you want to remove the barrier? Lazarus died four days ago. By this time there is a stench."

Jesus boldly answered her and said, "Martha, didn't I tell you if you believed you would see the glory of God?"

Martha knew Jesus was "I Am." Doubt didn't exist when she shared her life with him. She thought, *He creates. He heals. He will raise my brother's lifeless body to life.*

So, they took away the stone and Jesus said in a loud voice, "Lazarus, come out." And Lazarus came out. He was bound from head to foot in grave cloth.

The crowd was stunned. Jesus finally relaxed and said to them, "Loose him and let him go."

Many of the religious people who came to comfort Mary and Martha were Pharisees. They had tried to seize Jesus in the temple. Most saw Jesus raise Lazarus from the dead, and believed Jesus was the Son of God. But some of them went away and told the other Pharisees the things Jesus did. Then the chief priests and the Pharisees gathered a council and said, "What shall we do. This man works many signs. If we leave him alone, everyone will believe in him, and the Romans will come and take away both our position and our nation."

Caiaphas, the high priest, said to them, "You have no idea what this man will accomplish. We must consider killing him. It is most expedient for us that one man should die for the people, otherwise the whole nation perishes."

The Pharisees agreed with Caiaphas. They commanded, "If anyone knows where Jesus is, report his location to us that we might seize him." From that day forward, they plotted to put Jesus to death.

Jesus knew their plan. He stopped walking openly among the people. He left Bethany, went into the country near the wilderness to a city called Ephraim and remained there with us.

Our God is truly an awesome God. His powers are mighty and unmatched. He created our world, He gives life, and He has conquered death.

The Father is disturbed by the heavy burden of pain we carry when we grieve. We do not weep alone. He is glorified in our sorrow when we fold into His arms and turn our troubles over to Him for safekeeping and resolution.

The Holy Spirit can bring new life to the most difficult situation. Do you believe this?

The Son of God also knows the pain we carry in our heart and mind. He sees what lies behind the boulders where we entomb our deepest sorrow and darkest memories. He loves us as we are, and Spirit weeps with us as we grieve.

Come to Jesus. His love for us is limitless and his problem-solving skills cannot be compared. When we remove the stones that hold back the harmful emotions we carry through life, Spirit will work with us to live clean in a new life.

Hosanna

John 12:1-43

Six days before the Passover, we traveled with Jesus to Bethany to attend a dinner given in his honor at Lazarus' home. When the people learned Jesus returned to Lazarus' home, a large crowd traveled from Jerusalem to see Jesus and Lazarus. Many put their faith in Jesus that night when they saw he raised Lazarus from the dead. When the chief priests heard the strength of Lazarus' testimony before the people, they made plans to kill him as well.

The next day we walked to Jerusalem. A great multitude came out to greet Jesus as he entered the city. The people called him their king. They spread palm branches on the ground and shouted, "Hosanna! Blessed is he who comes in the name of the Lord. Blessed is the King of Israel."

The people who saw Jesus raise Lazarus from the dead heard the crowd and spread the word throughout the city that the man who performed this miracle had arrived in town. Many more people left their homes and work places to stand along the streets to see Jesus.

God's Son did not disappoint this massive gathering. He found a young donkey, and rode it into Jerusalem, as it is written, "Do not be afraid, O Daughter of Zion. See, your king is coming, seated on a donkey."

Jesus loved the people with the love of God, and the people praised their new King of Israel, Jesus Christ. This was Jesus' triumphant entry.

The Pharisees watched the spectacle in the Jerusalem streets and said to one another, "See, our plan is getting us nowhere. Look how the whole world has gone after him!"

We were beside ourselves with joy. Our Messiah was finally receiving the glory and honor he deserved from his people. After today's spectacle, we felt certain Jesus would finally establish his earthly kingdom.

Peter and I walked beside each other as we followed Jesus through the crowded streets. I said, "Peter, can you imagine the crowd at the temple courtyard tomorrow? Jesus could be made King of Israel."

Peter glanced at me and said, "John, we never know what tomorrow will bring. Let's enjoy this triumph while it lasts."

Later that day, several Greeks came to Philip and asked to see Jesus. Philip said to them, "Let me ask if the Rabbi is available." Philip turned to Andrew with the request and they both went to Jesus.

When Jesus heard the petition, he stepped away from all of us and went to meet the Greeks. Along the way, a crowd congregated around him, so he stopped and began to teach about his impending death.

Jesus spoke with authority, saying, "The time has come for the Son of Man to be glorified in death. Do not be sad when I leave you. I shall return. I am like the kernel of wheat that falls to the ground. Unless the kernel dies, it remains a single seed. If it dies, it raises from the ground in new life as many seeds.

"As I have taught you before, the man who loves his life and lives in darkness is condemned. He loses his life when this life ends. The one who is born of Spirit follows me to new life and never perishes but lives to eternal life. If you have an ear, hear. Whoever serves me must follow me, and where I am, they will also be. My Father will honor the ones that follow me. Hear my voice and follow me."

Jesus was emotional as he looked across the throng of people. "I tell you the truth. I am troubled at the thought of leaving you. What shall I say then? Let this hour pass for me? No, every sign I have performed and every word I have spoken to you has pointed to this day. I say, Father, glorify your name!"

When Jesus finished speaking these words, a voice came from above, and said, "I have glorified my name and I will glorify it again." The crowd heard the voice. Some said it was thunder. Others said an angel spoke to Jesus.

Jesus said, "My Father spoke to me for your benefit. My Father is with me and I am with my Father. Now is the time for judgement. The prince of darkness will be driven out of this world by my Father. When the world lifts me from the earth, I will draw all men to myself."

The crowd spoke up then and said, "We heard from the law that the Christ will remain forever. How can you say you are the Son of Man and you will be crucified? Who is this Son of Man who will stay with us to rule the kingdom of the Jews forever?"

Even after Jesus performed all the miraculous signs, the crowd still did not believe in him. Yet many of the religious leaders did believe in Jesus. They feared the Pharisees, so they kept their belief to themselves. They knew if they confessed their faith in Jesus as the Son of God, they would be put out of the synagogue. They needed their jobs. Their work provided status and income. Could they trust God for their daily existence?

Jesus was disappointed when he heard the crowd's question, but he wasn't surprised. He knew their hearts and minds. He didn't explain plainly to them about the Son of Man's resurrection and his life after death. Instead, he reminded them of this important spiritual truth. He said, "You have me for a little longer. Believe in me before the darkness overcomes you. The man who walks in the dark doesn't know where he is going. Put your trust in me before you are lost in the deep black and you can't find your way back."

When he finished speaking, he left and hid himself from the people.

Jesus suffered emotional hardship at the hands of the crowd and the religious people throughout his ministry. He was disappointed and saddened by the crowd's rejection and angered by the Pharisees hypocrisy. Yet he and his disciples actively engaged the people with the Father's miraculous signs and words throughout Judea, Galilee, and Samaria for three years.

It is easy to pack our bags and look for an opportunity to escape the kind of verbal abuse and active rejection Jesus and the disciples endured from the people. Jesus walked away from some people once he knew their hearts and minds, but he didn't walk away from the life he was given to live on earth by his Father. On the last days of his public life, he was moved to deep sadness at the thought of leaving these people. He loved them as the one who gives eternal life.

How did Jesus prosper in strength and integrity during this challenging life to love so deeply those who were so unlovable? Jesus did not walk alone. He didn't depend on these people for emotional security. Jesus shared his heart-of-hearts with his Father and his disciples, and he loved the unlovable people from the overflow of his love for God.

Jesus knew why he was here. He came to the people that they might have life and love and have it abundantly.

Before we walk into an emotionally charged situation, make sure we stand in the Light before darkness overcomes us. Trust Spirit and He will show us the way to love and live. When we follow Spirit, we can love the unlovable from the overflow of our love for God. We are not responsible for how we are loved and liked in return.

The Last Supper

John 13:1-38

The evening sun closed across the Jerusalem sky as religious people entered their homes to eat their Passover meal. We all came to the upper room we rented earlier in the day and prepared to share our meal together. Jesus sat back and thought about how much he loved us as our evening meal was being served.

When everyone was comfortable and engaged in light dinner conversation, Jesus rose from his place at the table. He took off his outer garment and wrapped a towel around his waist. Then he filled a basin with water and began to wash our feet.

When he finished washing all the disciples' feet, he put on his clothes and returned to his place at the table. He smiled softly as he sat down and then he said, "Do you understand what I have done for you? I have set an example. We have lived together for three years. You will be blessed if you do for others as I have done for you during our time together.

"You call me Teacher and Lord, and you are right to call me those names because I am your leader. True leaders naturally display a servant's heart. Live your life as I have lived before you."

As the evening progressed, Jesus' countenance changed, and his eyes saddened. It was obvious to everyone in the room his spirit was troubled as he began to speak. He said, "One of you will betray me tonight."

We were all stunned by his words. We stared at each other in confusion. Each disciple was at a loss to whom Jesus meant.

I sat next to Jesus, so Peter motioned to me to ask Jesus who would betray him. I leaned toward Jesus and asked the question. Jesus broke off a piece of bread and said, "It is the one to whom I will give this piece of bread when I've dipped it in the dish." Shortly thereafter, Jesus handed the bread to Judas

Iscariot, and said, "Judas, do what you are about to do, quickly." As soon as Judas took the bread, Satan entered Judas, and he went out into the night.

After Judas departed, Jesus leaned forward and began to talk to all of us in the upper room as a loving father speaks to his children. He said, "This is our last evening together for a while. Where I am going you cannot go. I have many important thoughts I want to share with you before I leave, so listen closely. The dark world hates me, and it will hate you. Therefore, I give you a new commandment. Do not walk away on your own when I leave. Love one another as I have loved you. The world will know you are my disciples if you love one another."

Peter stood up from his place at the table. I saw the tears pool in his eyes as he asked Jesus, "Lord, where are you going?"

Jesus leaned back to look at Simon Peter and said, "Peter, listen to me. I have given you a new commandment tonight. Love your brothers. You need each other. Where I go tomorrow, you cannot go now. But Peter, you will follow me later."

Peter shook his head and began to argue with Jesus in his fisherman's way. He asked, "Lord, why can't I follow you now? I'm ready to lay down my life for you."

Jesus gazed at Peter with a tender heart and said, "Simon Peter, you have no idea what I'm about to face and still you have spoken well. You will minister to these same people. A day will come at the end of your mighty ministry, when you will lay down your life for me. Now is not that day.

"I tell you the truth, I know you love me, but you will deny me three times before the rooster crows tomorrow morning. Peter, do not walk away to live by yourself when I leave. Love your brothers as I have loved you."

Our world turns topsy-turvy when the people we love the most are taken away. Our heart breaks when we realize we can't keep them with us. We are lost without them. They leave us with dreams unfulfilled. We want to follow them where they go, but this life will not allow us to go after them.

What happens when our world begins to spin out of control with painful sorrow? We are numb, confused, and depressed. How do we fill the jagged hole that's ripped from our heart to our soul? How can we endure painful loss with strength we do not possess? Do we take our eyes off Spirit to mask our pain with worldly answers? Do we allow the Prince of Darkness to snuff out the Light of Life we've followed? Does he destroy our joy and what is good in God's sight?

The night before his death, Jesus said to his disciples, "Do not let your hearts be troubled and do not be afraid. Trust God and trust Me."

God gifts us with the grieving process to heal our pain. Trust Spirit to guide us through this emotionally trying time to its positive end. Don't walk away on your own to suffer sorrow by yourself. Open your broken heart and allow the Father to love you during the quiet moments. Then find a way to love those who are closest to you, the same way Jesus loves you. They grieve too.

The Ministry Begins Anew

John 15:18-27, 16:1-4, 14:1-31

Peter took his place at the table and sat down with his brothers. Many in the room wondered what tomorrow would bring and how they might react if Simon Peter could deny Jesus three times before sunrise.

Jesus knew their thoughts and their hearts. He looked around the table to reassure each person, then he said, "Do not let your heart be troubled and do not be afraid. Trust God and trust me. You have been with me since the beginning. My Father will send you Spirit who will tell others about me through you. You must speak for me because you know me better than anyone else. If the world hates you, remember it hated me first. Rest assured, if I am persecuted, you will also be persecuted. The world will treat you this way because of my name."

Jesus stopped for a moment to allow the disciples to absorb his words. When he saw their eyes were riveted to him, he said, "I tell you all this, so you won't wander off when the hardship begins. The religious people will put you out of the synagogue. In fact, the time will come when anyone who kills you will believe he is doing God a service. They do this because they do not know the Father or me. I did not tell you this earlier because I lived with you. Starting tomorrow, you must walk together as one without me. I tell you again, do not walk away on your own when I leave. You know me. Love one another as I have loved you. The world will know you are my disciples if you love one another as I love you."

Jesus opened his hands to his disciples then and said, "You wonder where I am going. I tell you; I leave you tomorrow to return to my Father in Heaven. I look forward to preparing a place for you where I go. When your time here ends, I will come back for you from Heaven and take you where I am, that we may be together again. Now you know where I go, and you know the way to the place I am going."

We listened to Jesus, but some of us did not understand him. Thomas spoke up and said to Jesus, "Lord, we don't know where you are going. How can we know the way to get there?"

Jesus answered Thomas and said, "I am the way, Thomas. I am also the truth and the light. Without me, no one can go to the Father. If you really knew me, you would know the Father and I are one. Look at me, Thomas. Do you see me? From now on, you know the Father and you have seen Him."

Philip interrupted Jesus and said, "Lord, show us the Father. That will be enough for us to stand for you in the trying times to come." (*This would be a fair question for anyone who saw Jesus with human eyes and understanding, especially when the world they knew was collapsing around them.*)

Jesus gazed at the people in the room with sympathetic eyes and answered Philip, saying, "Philip, you've faithfully walked with me since the second day. We've been together for three years. Don't you know me by now? Think about the mighty miracles you've seen and the powerful words you've heard spoken by me in love with mercy and truth. Do you really believe they just came from me? Philip, God is Spirit. The Father lives in me and He does His work through me. If you have seen me, you have seen the Father in my works and you have heard Him in my words. If you know me, you know the Father. We are one."

When Jesus finished speaking to Philip, he turned his attention to everyone in the room. He said, "Do not believe what you see in the coming days. Keep your faith in me and be patient during the dark days ahead. They will not last. I promise I will not leave you as orphans. The world will not see me again after tomorrow, but you will see me. When I am raised from the dead, I will come to you. Because I live again, you shall not perish, but have everlasting life. When you see me, the words I speak to you tonight will ring true. You will realize that I am in my Father, you are in me, and I am in you."

Judas (not Judas Iscariot) spoke up then and said, "Lord, I don't understand why you have to leave us. You are the Messiah. Why don't you show yourself to the world when you rise from the dead? The time has come to establish your earthly kingdom. Why just show yourself to us?"

Jesus shook his head and said to everyone, "My Father and I created the world and everything that has been made in it. Our kingdom is in Heaven. My Father did not send me here to rule an earthly kingdom. My Father loves His creation so much that he sent me here as His sacrifice for people's sin. The people who carry out my teachings love me, and the Father loves them. Whoever the Father loves, I will love, and I will show myself to them."

I spoke up then. "Lord, what else can we do? We will gladly do all you ask of us. But how can we testify on your behalf when you leave us? We are mere men. You are the Son of God, and the world does not understand you."

Jesus looked at each of us and said, "The Spirit of truth is coming to you. You have seen the power of the Holy Spirit work in me. I will leave it with you forever. You will know Spirit because He will live with you and will be in you. The Holy Spirit will teach you all things and will remind you of everything I have said to you. The ministry we have started together begins anew tomorrow. Believe me when I tell you, you will do greater works than me with Spirit when I go to the Father. You can ask me for anything in my name, and I will do it that the Son may bring glory to the Father through you."

Jesus stood up then in a calm and collected manner and said, "Peace I leave you. My peace I give to you. Do not let your hearts be troubled by what you hear and do not be afraid of what you see. Come with me now. It's time to leave."

The disciples were great men of courage and stamina. Their faith in God was unshakeable. Jesus was not leaving them to minister in a playground of love. He called them to battle in spiritual warfare, where lives were taken for loving and serving him.

On Jesus' last night with the disciples, he promised those who loved him, he would not leave them orphans. And he didn't. The disciples were not orphaned, and neither are we. Just because the Father and Son remain in Heaven does not mean God's children are condemned to live a lonely life surrounded by unbelief. The Father's children are born of Spirit; the same Spirit of truth the Father sent to Jesus' disciples when the Son of God ascended to Heaven.

We love Jesus and want to follow his commandments. What else can we do for him? We will gladly do all he asks of us. But how can we successfully testify on his behalf to a dark world where so many are set against godly ways?

Like the disciples, we are simply people. Jesus is the Son of God, and the world did not believe him. How will the dark world we walk in everyday believe us? If there is an answer, it begins with Spirit and credibility.

Jesus had credibility to teach because of the works he performed in his daily life. His actions and his words pointed to God.

God's children live with godly credibility before others through Spirit. The Holy Spirit teaches us all things when we listen for His voice, then follow His way, before our world, with love, mercy, and truth.

God did not send His Son to convert the world to a new religion. Jesus came to illuminate the dark world of unbelief. His actions and words pointed to God. What more can we do?

Love Each Other

John 15:1-17

We gathered at the bottom of the stairs to the upper room. When Jesus joined us, we began to walk the streets of Jerusalem to the Mount of Olives.

We were all quiet for a time, then Jesus began to teach as we passed a vineyard. He pointed to the healthy vines and said, "Look, the vinedresser has cut off the dead branches and pruned back the healthy branches from the vine. Why does the vinedresser clean every branch on the vine, Thomas?"

Thomas moved beside Jesus and replied, "So the vine will grow and bear more fruit, Lord."

Jesus turned his head toward Thomas then and said, "You speak well, Thomas. Look at the pile of brush on the side of the road. See the healthy branches mixed in with the withered branches? What happens to all the branches when they are removed from the vine?"

Thomas said, "Lord, it's dark out, but I can still see that all the branches wither and die when they are separated from the vine. How does this apply to us, Rabbi?"

Jesus stopped walking and we gathered around him as he began to speak. He said, "Think of me as the true vine, my Father as the vinedresser, and my Father's children as the vine's branches. My Father takes away every branch that does not bear fruit and He will prune every healthy branch that does bear fruit, so the vine will grow and bear more fruit."

Peter interrupted Jesus and said, "Lord, I remember when you healed the blind man outside the temple. You said a hard thing for us to understand when we asked who sinned. You said, 'No one sinned. This happened to the man that the work of God might be seen in his life.' Is this an example of the Father pruning a man?"

Jesus smiled and then he said, "Yes, Peter. And what we each face in the coming hours and days is also pruning.

"Take a look at that pile of rubbish. No branch bears fruit unless it is joined with the vine. In the same way, you can't live with Spirit unless you remain with me. Apart from me, you can do nothing with Spirit or the Father. If anyone chooses to leave me, they are like the branch that is thrown away and withers. They are picked up and thrown into the fire to be burned. If you choose to stay with me, keep my words close to your heart while the Prince of Darkness has his way in the world. Ask whatever you wish, and it will be given to you. My Father will be glorified during the dark days as you bear much fruit."

Jesus began to move then. We followed as he talked to us. He said, "I love you with the same love I love my Father. My love will always remain with you and your joy will be complete if you follow my commandments. This is my new commandment: Love each other as I love you. Greater love has no one than he lay down his life for his friends. You shall see very soon that my love for my Father is the greatest love."

Jesus turned around for a moment to look at us. He smiled softly, and said, "I remember when you each came to me as disciples. You did not choose me. I chose you. Now I appoint you to go back into the world I leave to live with the Holy Spirit, and bear much fruit. Do not be afraid. The Father will give you whatever you ask for in my name, and He will be glorified through your works and your words."

This is Jesus' command to us: Love each other as I love you.

Mount of Olives

John 16:5-33

We arrived at the Mount of Olives and sat down to rest at our usual place. When we settled in our sorrow, Jesus said, "You are filled with grief because I tell you I am leaving you. There is more you must hear. Like me, you will also face a society that hates you and persecutes you. I understand your sadness is deep. These are hard words for anyone to accept.

"I love you as I love my Father. You must trust me now. It is in your best interest that I go away. Spirit cannot come to you until I send Him. I have so much more to tell you tonight, but I can see you are exhausted by the words I've already shared with you. Don't worry. When Spirit comes, He will guide you to all truth. He will not speak His own words. Spirit will bring glory to me by taking what is mine and making it known to you."

Jesus stepped away from us then. We could see through his eyes the deep love he shared for us. His heart was shaken with sadness by the realization the time he shared with us was quickly coming to an end. When he regained his composure, he stepped toward us and said, "You will not see me in a little while, but then you will see me again in a little while."

Some disciples were confused by Jesus' vague language. They didn't understand what Jesus meant when he said, "You will not see me in a little while, but then you will see me again in a little while."

They kept asking each other, "What does he mean by 'a little while'? We don't understand what the Rabbi is saying."

Jesus saw we were exhausted with sorrow and confused by his words, so he said to us, "Now is the time for grief, my friends. You will weep and mourn for a short time while the world rejoices at my death. You grieve now, but believe me as I say to you, do not lose heart. Your grief will turn to joy. You will see me again and no one will take away your joy. On that day, you will no longer need to ask me for anything. You can ask the Father in my name and you will receive what you request. On that day, your joy will be complete.

"I have spoken to you with vague language, but when I come back to you, I will speak plainly to you about my Father."

All the disciples raised their eyes to Jesus then and some said, "Lord, please speak plainly to us now."

Jesus returned the disciples gaze and answered them, saying, "Alright, my friends. I came from my Father and entered the world; now I am leaving the world and going back to the Father."

We looked toward each other and shook our heads with gladness, then returned our gaze to Jesus and said, "Lord, thank you for speaking clearly. Now we believe you came from God and you know all things."

This sounds like an odd profession of faith three years into the disciples' ministry with the Son of God. Remember where they sit and what they face in the coming hours. They believe they will die tonight with their leader, yet no one runs. They simply wanted to hear the assurance that their faith was justified in plain language.

The disciples witnessed Jesus heal the sick, blind, and lame. They saw him raise a man from the dead. They helped him feed five thousand men and their families with five loaves of bread and two fish. They saw him walk on water and calm the sea. They witnessed him clear the temple with a whip of cords. They heard him speak to multitudes like no man before him. And now they waited with him on the Mount of Olives to suffer their death at the hands of the religious elite.

The disciples' last days with Jesus were an emotional roller coaster. They went from a time of joy and celebration at Jesus' triumphant entry into Jerusalem to a time of exhausting grief on the Mount of Olives.

We are never prepared to face hard stops in our life. They will normally come to us like a thief in the night to steal our joy, peace, and security. Jesus tells us, "We will face trouble in this world, but take heart, I have overcome the world."

When life trauma stops the trajectory of our life, embrace the time for grief. Weep and mourn, but do not lose heart. Let grief follow its healing path to joy as Spirit lives with us through the dark time to new life.

Jesus Prays

John 17:1-26

Jesus stared into the night. He saw Judas with a detachment of soldiers and officials from the chief priests and Pharisees preparing to leave the temple to arrest him. His time had come. He became sorrowful and troubled. His soul was overwhelmed with sadness to the point of death.

Jesus gathered us together as one and gave us a long hug, and then he said, "I must talk to my Father now. Stay here and pray you will not fall into temptation. The spirit is willing, but the body is weak. Peter, James, and John, come with me while I pray to the Father."

Jesus walked a stone's throw from his other disciples then fell to his knees. He began to pray for himself, saying, "Father, the time has come to conquer death for mankind's sin. Honor Your Son through this overwhelming experience so I may glorify you. You granted me authority over all people that I might gift eternal life to everyone you give me. I am ready to complete the work you have given me to do on earth, but Father I need you right now. Please honor me by your presence with the glory I had before the world began."

We were exhausted with grief. Everyone slept while I sat to the side and watched over our leader. The moment Jesus prayed for his Father's presence, I saw what appeared to be an angel come to Jesus and minister to his needs. When Jesus was strengthened, he began to pray for the disciples. He said, "Father, these men were yours. You gave them to me from this world. They accept and obey your word and know with certainty I come from you. I pray for the disciples, Father, because they are yours. I am not praying for the dark world, but for these men you have given me. I am coming to you, but these men remain in the world. Protect them and keep them safe by the power of Your name—the name you have given me—so they may be one, as You and I are one. I am not asking you to take them out of the world. I pray you will protect them from the Evil One as I send them into the world. Father, they are not of this world any more than I am of this world. I pray you will separate them from the world with your truth. Your word is truth."

Jesus came back to the other disciples then and found them all asleep. He stood among them for a few minutes then he returned to his place and began to pray for all believers to come. He said, "Father, my prayer is for all those who will believe in me through the disciples' ongoing message. May they be one, as you and I are one. May they be in complete unity to show the world You sent me, and You love them as You love me. Father, when their time comes, I want those You have given me to be with me where I am. I want them to see the honor You have given me because You loved me before the world was created.

"Holy Father, the world does not know You, but I know You, and the disciples know You have sent me. I have made You known to them. I will continue to make You known to them, so that the love You have for me may be in them and I myself may be in them."

The Prince of Darkness was prepared to collapse on Jesus to take his life and discredit his ministry. Jesus began to be sorrowful and troubled as his final hour with his disciples neared. His soul was overwhelmed with sadness to the point of death. He turned to the one place he could find relief from his grief, and the strength to face his darkest day with grace and mercy. He talked with his Father. What were the priorities Jesus shared with the Father for himself, His disciples, and his church as he prepared to leave the earth and return to the Father?

For himself, he asked His Father to honor him so Jesus could glorify his Father through this overwhelming experience. For the disciples, he asked the Father to protect them from the Evil One by the power of his name. He also asked the Father to separate them from the world with his truth as Jesus sent them into the world. For the church, he asked his Father that all believers be one, as the Father and Son are one. When the time comes for believers to leave this life, Jesus asked the Father that they be with him where he is, so they can see the honor his Father has given him.

Our greatest gift in life is knowing we have a Father in Heaven who loves us as His children. He knows us by name, and He listens to us when we call out to Him in the name of Jesus Christ. Words aren't important to Him since

He knows our heart and mind and loves us where we stand. We can come to Him as we are, in joy or sorrow. If we enter His throne room with a heart of praise and thanksgiving, we will feel His majesty and realize our Father is greater than all.

He protects us from the Evil One as He separates us from the world with His truth. No one can snatch us from His hand. He is the great "I AM" Who can stand against Him when we live in the intimacy of the light He shines before us?

If the world hates us and persecutes us for His name's sake, does it matter? We have passed from death to abundant life with the Holy Spirit. One day we will enter the Kingdom of God and move on to eternal life where we will see Jesus in his glory.

Peter Wept Bitterly

John 18:1-27

Judas Iscariot knew Jesus prayed with his men at an olive grove across from the Kidron Valley. Jesus knew Judas was guiding a group of armed soldiers to arrest him at that location. When Jesus finished his prayer, he woke up the other disciples and we left to cross the Kidron Valley and proceed to the olive grove.

The time for talk was over. Each man walked with his own thoughts. I stayed beside Jesus. Peter walked on the other side with his hand resting on his sword's hilt. The other disciples remained close. Each man was committed to surrender his life to protect the Messiah.

The night was dark. We watched the torches travel toward us before we observed the men carrying them. When Jesus saw Judas enter the olive grove, he stepped away from us and called out to the group of men in a strong voice. He asked, "Who do you seek?"

They said, "We seek Jesus of Nazareth."

Jesus stepped closer to them and said, "I am Jesus of Nazareth."

When Jesus' words reached the mob, Judas, the soldiers, and the religious leaders all drew back in fear and fell to the ground. Jesus shook his head in amazement as he walked forward. He extended a helping hand to the men on the ground and asked them again, "Who is it you want?"

The commanding officer got to his feet, arranged his equipment, and then said with trepidation, "We want Jesus of Nazareth."

Jesus answered the man and said, "I told you that I am he. If you want me, then let my disciples go."

The religious leader stepped forward then and answered Jesus. He said, "We came for you. Your disciples mean nothing to us. They can go their own way when we take you."

Peter charged past Jesus then and attacked Judas' group with his sword. He cut off the right ear of the high priest's servant before Jesus could grab his sword hand.

When Jesus had Peter under physical control He said, "Peter, put your sword away before you cause more harm. Shall I not drink from the cup my Father has given me?"

When the situation stabilized, the detachment of soldiers and the religious officials arrested our leader. There was nothing we could do to help him. They bound Jesus like a common criminal in the dark of night and took him to Annas, the father-in-law of Caiaphas, the other high priest.

Peter and I followed Jesus to the high priest's courtyard. I knew Annas, so the gatekeeper allowed me to follow Jesus inside the gate. Peter remained outside the entrance until I received permission for him to enter the courtyard. When Peter passed through, a girl on duty at the gate pointed to Jesus and asked Peter, "Aren't you one of his disciples?"

Peter did not stop to answer the girl. He mumbled to her as he passed and said, "I am not." When he cleared the gate, he hurried toward an open fire the servants and officials maintained to keep warm. Peter didn't look for me and he didn't draw near to Jesus. He stayed by the fire with the servants and the officials.

Jesus had everyone's attention, so it was easy for me to stay reasonably close to him without causing a problem for my Lord or myself. Jesus stood with bound hands before Annas as he was interrogated about his disciples and his teaching.

At one point Jesus finally said, "I have spoken openly to the world. I have said nothing in secret. I always taught in the synagogues and the temple where all the religious people come together. Why question me here? Ask those around you tonight who heard me teach. Surely they know what I said."

When he made this statement, an official who stood nearby doubled his fist and struck Jesus in the face with a hard blow. When he drew his hand back to strike again, the official said, "Is this any way to speak to the high priest?"

Jesus took a moment to regain his composure. He spit blood from his mouth, then he talked plainly to Annas, saying, "If I have said something wrong, tell me what is wrong. But if I speak the truth, why do you strike me?"

Annas looked Jesus in the eyes and simply shook his head. This interrogation was not about truth. Everyone knew the truth. Jesus was sent by

God to the Jews. This was about protecting the religious elite. This group of men decided it would be good for the nation if this man died for the people.

Simon Peter stayed by the fire as Jesus endured his ordeal with Annas. As he made himself comfortable by the fire, a man asked him if he was a disciple. Peter denied it, saying, "I am not."

One of the high priest's servants, a relative of the man whose ear was cut off, challenged Peter. He said, "Didn't I see you at the olive grove?"

Again, Peter denied it, and at that moment a rooster began to crow. Jesus turned and looked straight at Simon Peter. When their eyes locked, Peter's spirit broke with shame.

He remembered the words his Lord spoke to him in the upper room: "Simon Peter, before the rooster crows in the morning, you will deny me three times."

Peter was a strong man who loved the Messiah deeply. Hours before, he attacked an entire detachment of soldiers by himself to protect Jesus. Now he failed to stand for Jesus when Jesus stood all alone.

Sometimes the spirit is willing, but the body is weak. Peter wept bitterly as he left the courtyard. We will disappoint the Father and those we love the most during our lifetime. How we respond to our transgressions defines our true character and molds our future behavior.

Peter wept bitterly in the dark of night. When he finished, he embraced remorse as a reminder that we pay a painful cost when we live apart. We compound our pain when we walk away to live alone with guilt and shame.

Leave the harmful emotions attached to our mistakes at the feet of our Savior who died for all sin. Forgive yourself and those around you, as the Father in Heaven forgives you. Then return to Spirit and begin anew as you make amends with those who have been harmed or disappointed.

Caiaphas

Matt 26:57-68, John 18:28-32

When Caiaphas, the high priest, had assembled the entire Sanhedrin, he sent word to Annas that the teachers of the law and the elders were ready to interrogate Jesus. These men were determined to obtain evidence they could use to have Jesus executed.

Jesus stood quietly before this assembly and listened to several witnesses give false testimony about him. No one gave information worthy of death. Finally, two witnesses came forward and testified they heard Jesus say, "I am able to destroy God's temple and rebuild it in three days."

Everyone looked to Jesus for a response, but he didn't answer the charge.

Caiaphas stood up and said to Jesus, "Aren't you going to answer the testimony these men bring against you?"

Jesus remained silent as he allowed his gaze to move around the room. He thought to himself, *The Pharisees asked me for a sign of my authority the day I cleared the temple with a whip of cords. The time has finally come for me to reveal my authority to the world.*

Jesus stood tall and continued to hold his gaze before the Sanhedrin as he thought, *You will kill me today as it has been foretold in scripture, but the world will know "I AM" when I rise from the dead in three days.*

Jesus frustrated Caiaphas. The high priest's scheme to obtain damning evidence was failing. Caiaphas left his seat in anger. He stood before Jesus and said, "Tell us under oath before the living God: Are you the Christ, the Son of God?"

Jesus nodded his head and said, "Yes, it is as you say. And I say to all of you, the day is coming when you will see me sitting at the right hand of the Mighty One, coming on the clouds of Heaven."

Jesus gave Caiaphas the evidence he sought with these spoken words. The high priest was beside himself. He tore his clothes in false anger and said to the Sanhedrin, "He has spoken blasphemy! What do you all think? Do we need more witnesses?"

The Sanhedrin replied as one as they stood up and moved toward Jesus. They said, "This man's words are worthy of death."

Many stepped forward to spit in Jesus' face and strike him with their fists. Others slapped him and said, "Prophesy to us, Christ. Who slapped you?" Jesus endured this beating with the strength of the Father who was in him.

All the chief priests and elders of the people decided to put Jesus to death early in the morning. They bound Jesus and led him to the palace of Pilate, the Roman governor. The governor came out of the palace to address the religious leaders. When he saw Jesus' battered face, he asked Caiaphas, "What charge do you bring against this man?"

The fact is, Jesus hadn't broken any Roman laws, especially a law deserving death. Caiaphas was stuck. His law did not permit him to execute Jesus because Jesus did not commit a civil crime deserving the death penalty.

Caiaphas attempted to brush over these facts by answering Pilate's question this way: "If he were not a criminal, we would not hand him over to you."

Pilate looked at Jesus and shook his head, then he placed his hand on Jesus' arm and guided him back toward the elders. He said, "The Roman government has no interest in this affair. Take him yourselves and judge him according to your laws."

Caiaphas started to panic when he heard Pilate's response. As Pilate turned his back on the religious elite and started to walk into the palace, Caiaphas raised his voice and called out, saying, "We need you. We have no right to execute anyone."

Pilate thought to himself, *These men need me on their side. What can be gained by offering my help?*

Small men planned to use their political influence to take down a righteous man who threatened their way of life.

Pilate

John 18:33-40, 19:1-16

Pilate was politically sophisticated. He recognized the advantage he'd gain taking Jesus off the religious leaders' hands. As Pilate stepped into his palace, he decided to summon Jesus for questioning. When the palace guards presented Jesus to him, the governor said, "I understand you are the King of the Jews. Am I entertaining the leader of the Jewish people?"

Jesus was beaten by the Sanhedrin, but he was not broken. He stood before the governor with his feet planted shoulder width apart. Jesus asked Pilate, "Is this your idea, or has someone else talked to you about me?"

Pilate answered Jesus and said, "Am I a Jew? Your people handed you over to me. Now tell me what you have done to the religious people that your leaders want me to put you to death? Are You King of the Jews?"

Pilate looked into Jesus' eyes and was drawn to the Spirit in Jesus. When Jesus spoke, the governor listened. Jesus said, "My kingdom is not of this world. If I came to establish my kingdom on earth, my servants would fight to prevent my arrest. For now, my kingdom is from another place."

Pilate smiled when he heard Jesus' response. He replied, "So then, you are a king."

Jesus gazed into the governor's eyes and then he said, "You are right to say I am a king. My kingdom is elsewhere. I was born and came into this world to testify to my Father's truth. Everyone on the side of truth listens to me."

Pilate's heart softened further as Jesus spoke to him. He asked Jesus, "What is truth?"

Jesus shared his truth with Pilate, then the governor went out to the religious leaders and said, "I find no basis for a charge against this man. It is your custom for me to release one prisoner to you at the time of the Passover. Do you want me to release the King of the Jews?"

The whole assembly of leadership rose up and shouted to Pilate, "Not him, we want Barabbas." Barabbas was a known criminal convicted of murder and of taking part in a rebellion against the Roman government. When Pilate heard their response, he shook his head in disbelief and went back into the palace.

The governor decided the best way to save Jesus' life was to severely punish him, then present him for release to the large crowd that was gathering in the palace courtyard. Surely, the people this man ministered to for three years would show compassion and want him returned to their lives. After all, these same people lined the streets, singing praises and naming this man, "King of Israel."

Pilate turned Jesus over to his soldiers to be flogged. The soldiers stripped him to his waist, tied him to a whipping post, and beat Jesus within an inch of his life with a whip fitted with a cat-of-nine-tails.

When the soldiers finished tearing his back to shreds, they twisted together a crown of thorns, forced it onto Jesus' head, and then clothed him in a purple robe. The soldiers mocked Jesus to amuse themselves. They said, "Hail, King of the Jews." Then they beat him about his head with their fists and a wooden staff.

When the soldiers finished their work, Jesus was hard to recognize. His body was broken, but his spirit was alive.

Jesus ultimately came to this world to face this day as a sacrifice for mankind's sin. He endured this torture by clinging to his love for our Father.

Tears formed in Pilates eyes when Jesus returned to him. Pilate's heart convicted him. He was not dealing with an ordinary man.

The governor went outside again to speak to the religious leaders. He was encouraged when he saw the crowd outside the palace had grown. Word had spread throughout Jerusalem that Jesus was on trial for his life. People who were formerly blind, lame, and sick mingled with those who witnessed Lazarus return from the dead. Many who lined the streets singing, "Hosanna! Blessed is he who comes in the name of the Lord! Blessed is the King of Israel," were present.

Pilate was confident Jesus' followers would choose to release him over Barabbas. He spoke to them in a loud voice, saying, "Look, I am bringing Jesus out to you. I have interrogated your king and severely punished him, but I find no basis for a charge against him. This man is innocent."

When Jesus came out dressed in the crown of thorns and purple robe, the people barely recognized the battered man. Those who loved the Son of God, began to chant, "Jesus, Jesus, Jesus."

When the chief priests and the crowd they controlled saw Jesus, they shouted, "Crucify! Crucify!" The religious people's voices drowned out the voices of those who loved the Messiah.

Pilate was dumbfounded. He spoke directly to the religious leaders and said, "You take him and crucify him. As for me, I find no basis for a charge against him."

The religious leaders refused to accept Pilate's word. They told him, "This man declared himself to be the Son of God. According to our law, this is blasphemy. Blasphemy is a sin punished by death. You must crucify him."

When Pilate heard Jesus declared he was the Son of God, fear gripped his heart. He brought Jesus back into the palace and he asked Jesus, "Where are you from?" Jesus looked at Pilate through slits in his swollen eyes, but he did not answer the governor.

Pilate moved toward Jesus then and said, "Why do you refuse to answer my question? Don't you realize I have the power to free you or crucify you?"

Jesus answered Pilate then and said, "The only power you have over me is given to you from above."

Pilate tried to set Jesus free, but the religious people kept shouting, "If you let this man go, you are no friend of Caesar's. Anyone who claims to be a king opposes Caesar."

Pilate asked them, "Shall I crucify your king?"

The chief priests answered, "We have no king but Caesar." Pilate finally gave up and washed his hands of the whole ordeal. He turned Jesus over to be crucified.

Pilate's instincts told him to turn Jesus away at the palace door. He sought a political advantage when he invited Jesus into the palace. The dark world used Pilate's ambition to place him in an indefensible position that cost Jesus his life.

God's children do not manipulate situations to honor themselves in the dark world. Evil will kill, steal, or destroy what God has created in us. God's children obey Spirit's voice and live in the open where their life is clearly seen.

Crucify Him

John 19:16-30, Matt 27:41-48

Pilate lost patience with the crowd when it turned into a mob. They wanted Barabbas. So Pilate released Barabbas to the people and he turned Jesus over to his soldiers.

The soldiers brought Jesus into the governor's official residence. They took off the purple robe but left the crown of thorns buried in his head. When Jesus finished dressing, the soldiers placed a wooden cross on his shoulder. The heavy post rested on his back's shredded flesh. The blood from his wounds immediately soaked through his shirt.

The cross probably weighed three hundred pounds. Jesus carried the wooden burden through Jerusalem's crowded streets to the place of the Skull, which is also called Golgotha.

Jesus pulled the cross up the incline to Golgotha's summit. When he reached his destination, he turned the cross over to the soldiers who waited for him. They laid the cross on the ground and nailed a notice Pilate prepared to the top of the cross. The sign read, "JESUS OF NAZARETH, KING OF THE JEWS." The notice was printed in three languages, Aramaic, Latin, and Greek. Many people read the sign because the place Jesus was crucified was near the city.

Jesus was beyond exhausted. He was numb with pain when the soldiers stripped him naked, then laid him on top of the cross. He was shocked with searing pain when the men stretched out his arm and drove a steel spike through the palm of his hand. It took all his courage to lay still while a soldier drove stakes into his other hand and his feet.

When Jesus was secured to the cross, the soldiers lifted him up and dropped the cross into a hole in the ground with a resounding thud. The force of the blow tore Jesus' flesh. Jesus pulled himself up with his hands to inhale and he dropped his full body weight onto his feet when he exhaled. Each breath caused agony.

Jesus suffered in silence.

I followed Jesus throughout this ordeal, along with his mother Mary, Mary's sister and Mary Magdalene. We stood together near the cross and were forced to listen to the chief priests, the elders, and the teachers of the law mock Jesus. These hate-filled men stood before a dying Jesus and said, "He saved others, but he can't save himself. He's the King of Israel. If he comes down from the cross, we will believe in him. He trusts in God. Let God rescue him since he's the Son of God." These religious men heaped insults on Jesus until the sixth hour when darkness came over all the land.

About the ninth hour, I heard Jesus cry out in a loud voice, saying, "My God, My God, why have you forsaken me?"

One of the men who heard Jesus cry out ran and got a sponge, filled it with wine vinegar and gave Jesus a drink. When Jesus received the drink, he said, "It is finished." With that, he lowered his head and gave up his spirit. A soldier came up to Jesus and drove a spear into his side to make sure Jesus was finished.

On this tragic day, an innocent man died a brutal death to sacrifice himself for all people's sin.

The Tomb

John 19:38-42, Matt 27:62-66

Joseph of Arimathea feared the religious elite. He was a secret follower of Jesus who kept his belief to himself until Jesus died on the cross. When Jesus gave up his spirit from his naked, pierced, and torn body, Joseph's world changed. His fear changed to righteous anger.

He went to the governor's palace by himself and asked Pilate for permission to bury Jesus. Pilate was pleased to grant Joseph his approval. When he received the documents he needed, Joseph went to the home of his friend, Nicodemus.

Nicodemus was the Pharisee who visited Jesus in the night. Joseph and Nicodemus secured seventy-five pounds of spices from Nicodemus's home, loaded it on a large cart, and walked to Golgotha.

They were devastated when they saw the Messiah.

The two men gently removed Jesus from the cross and placed him on the cart. There was a garden with a new tomb near the place Jesus was crucified. The two men laid Jesus in the new tomb and began to prepare his body for burial with the mixture of myrrh and aloes Nicodemus brought. They wrapped his body with the spices in strips of linen which was the Jewish custom.

When they finished, Nicodemus looked at Jesus' wrapped body and thought to himself, *Lord, I believe you are the Son of God. You told us, 'Destroy this temple, and I will raise it again in three days.' I believe you. They destroyed your body today. I look forward to seeing you again in three days.*

When Nicodemus completed his thought, both men left Jesus and rolled a large stone across the mouth of the tomb.

The next day, the chief priests and Pharisees returned to the governor's palace to speak with Pilate. When they gained an audience with him, they said, "We remember the deceiver saying, 'I will rise again after three days.' We need you to give an order to secure the tomb until the third day. There is a chance his disciples will come in the night and steal his body, then tell the people he rose from the dead. This deception will be worse than the first."

Pilate was still upset with these men. He wouldn't forget the fiasco they created at his expense. The governor looked at them and laughed as he thought, *Are your problems with the 'Son of God' ending or just beginning?*

Pilate answered then and said, "Do you really believe a guarded tomb will hold the Son of God when he rises from the dead?"

The religious leaders answered emphatically, "He will not rise."

Pilate laughed again and said, "We shall all see, won't we? In the meantime, take a guard and make the tomb as secure as you know how. We don't want anyone to say his disciples came in the night and stole his body, do we?"

Even if Jesus had died on a cross and remained in a tomb, he should be remembered as a great teacher sent from God. His life teaching should form a religion that is no better or worse than all other religions developed around dead men who have influenced people with their enlightened words and works.

The unique power found in the written word of Jesus' life is this: Jesus Christ died for our sins. He rose from the dead, ascended to Heaven, and still sends the Holy Spirit to live in us and with us.

We worship a living God in spirit and truth through the Son of God who sits at the right hand of our Father in Heaven. God's love is completed in us as we love others with His love.

Empty Tomb

John 20:1-18

On the third day, Mary Magdalene walked to the tomb before sunrise. When she arrived, the tomb was open. Strips of linen laid on the floor and Jesus' body was gone.

She was terrified.

She ran back to the home where the disciples stayed to find Peter and me. She was trembling when she saw us. She said, "I've been to the tomb. They have taken the Lord and I don't know where they have put him. Please come with me and see."

Peter and I left the house and ran to the tomb. I arrived first. I stood at the mouth of the tomb and saw the linen strips lying on the floor. When Peter entered the tomb, he saw the linen strips, as well as the burial cloth that had been wrapped around Jesus' head. The burial cloth was folded separately from the other cloth.

I entered the tomb then. Based on what I saw, I believed Jesus had risen from the dead.

Peter and I were both filled with joy as we returned to our homes. Jesus had risen from the dead! The words Jesus spoke to us at the Mount of Olives rang true: "Now is the time for grief, my friends. You will weep and mourn for a time while the world rejoices at my death. You grieve now, but believe me as I say to you, do not lose heart. Your grief will turn to joy. You will see me again and no one will take away your joy."

Mary Magdalene walked back to the tomb by herself. She stood outside and cried. While she wept, she bent over and looked inside. Mary was surprised when she saw two angels sitting where Jesus' body had been.

The angels asked her why she was sad. Mary said, "Someone has taken my Lord, and I do not know where they put him." When she finished answering the angels, she heard someone behind her. She assumed the gardener had arrived to begin his work.

The man asked her, "Why do you cry? Who is it you look for?"

She said, "I am looking for my Lord who was laid in this tomb. Sir, if you carried him away, please tell me where you put him, and I will get him."

Jesus gazed into her tear-stained eyes and simply said, "Mary." Mary's heart quickened when she recognized Jesus' voice.

She cried out, "Teacher," and fell to the ground to worship Jesus. She wrapped herself in a tight embrace around Jesus' feet and lower legs.

Jesus laughed with joy, then he said to his devoted friend, "Mary be careful. Do not hold onto me, for I have not yet returned to the Father. Go instead to my brothers and tell them I am returning to my Father and your Father and my God and your God."

Mary Magdalene walked home with a joyful heart. She kept thinking to herself, *The Messiah is alive. He's risen from the dead. Praise be to God on high. We worship a great and mighty God who is true to His word.*

With a jubilant step, Mary entered the home where the disciples were staying. She shared her great news, saying, "I have seen the Lord this morning!"

Everyone in the house stopped what they were doing and came to Mary with great anticipation. They asked her, "What did he say?"

Mary said, "He told me to tell you, 'I am returning to my Father and your Father and my God and your God.'"

The Messiah is alive. He died for our sins, conquered death, and rose from the dead. Jesus is the Christ, The Son of God. Praise be to God on high for the gift of abundant life today, and then life everlasting.

We worship a great and mighty Savior who is true to his word. Jesus will return to his Father and our Father and his God and our God to pour out the Holy Spirit on the Children of God.

Come and see.

Believe

John 20:19-29

As night approached on the third day, we all gathered with the doors locked because we feared the religious elite. We sat together discussing the words Jesus spoke to us at the Mount of Olives and made plans for the next day when Jesus appeared before us. He entered the house without accessing a door.

Jesus greeted us and said, "Peace be with you!"

Peter, Mary, and I had each told everyone Jesus had risen from the dead, but it was still hard for us to believe what our eyes were seeing.

After Jesus spoke his greeting, he showed us his hands and his side. The man who stood before us was the Son of God, risen from the dead.

The tension left the room for the first time since the last supper. Grief spilled from the people's hearts and we began to laugh with gladness as the stress left our bodies. The Messiah we followed for three years was alive! Jesus shared in our joy with us.

When everyone in the room calmed down and simply rejoiced in our heart, Jesus began to teach us about our future with kind words of encouragement.

As the time came for him to depart, he said again, "Peace be with you! As the Father sent me, I am sending you." And with that he breathed on us and said, "Receive the Holy Spirit. If you forgive anyone their sins, they are forgiven; if you do not forgive them, they are not forgiven."

Thomas wasn't in the house when Jesus came to us. When Thomas arrived, everyone gathered around him and rejoiced. We shared the good news, saying, "Thomas, Jesus is alive. We have seen the Lord!"

Thomas was in a dark mood. Grief overwhelmed him. Try as he might, people's happiness did not make him happy. People's joy did not bring him joy.

When he heard Jesus was alive, he said to his friends, "Unless I see the nail marks in his hands, put my fingers where the nails were, and put my hand in his side, I will not believe."

There was no point arguing with his disbelief. We stepped away from Thomas and rejoiced in this godly miracle without him. I thought to myself, *If Jesus wants to make himself known to Thomas, then he will in his own way and in his own time.*

A week later, we were in the house again, and Thomas was with us. The doors were locked, and again Jesus came and stood before us. He said, "Peace be with you!"

Thomas was overwhelmed with emotion. His Lord was alive! Tears pooled in his eyes as Jesus walked up to him.

Jesus said to Thomas, "See my hands? Place a finger in the nail holes, Thomas. See my side? Place your hand in my side. Thomas, the time to grieve is over. The time to rejoice begins. Stop doubting and believe. There is much work to do in the days to come."

Thomas was speechless.

He worshiped the Lord where he stood and finally said, "My Lord and my God."

Jesus loved Thomas with his eyes, and then he said, "Thomas, you believe because you have seen me. Blessed are those who will not see me and still believe."

Imagine the disciples' thoughts and emotions as they absorbed the fact Jesus had risen from the dead and appeared before them. This was a mighty man. This man conquered death.

God's Son left the tomb and stood with his disciples in their home. Jesus honored their unrelenting faith in his word and proved he is the risen Savior.

The faithful followers' spirits filled with overwhelming joy and their hearts and minds were consumed with awe-filled respect for the Father and the Son.

The disciples believed with unwavering faith because they saw Jesus. Blessed are we who will not see Jesus and still believe.

It's Jesus

John 21:1-25, 20:30-31, I Corinthians 13:1-8

I stood outside the house one afternoon with Peter, James, Thomas, Nathaniel and two other disciples. Simon Peter was fidgety. He needed to keep busy, so he said to us, "I'm going fishing." No one had a better plan, so we followed Peter to his boat.

We stayed all night and didn't catch a fish. In the early hours of morning, while it was still dark, we saw a man start a fire on the shore.

When the sun broke the horizon, the man called out to us and said, "Have you caught any fish?"

We replied, "No luck tonight. We didn't catch a single fish."

The man shook his head to agree, then said, "Throw your net to the right side of the boat and you will find what you seek."

Nathaniel said, "We just fished the right side."

I said to Nathaniel, "Just do it."

When we cast our net, it filled so full of fish we couldn't pull the net in the boat.

I turned to Peter and said, "It's Jesus."

Peter put on his outer garment, smiled at me, then jumped in the water and swam to shore.

When everyone arrived on land, we saw fish and bread cooking on a fire of burning coals. The man said, "Bring me some of the fish you have caught."

Peter ran back to his boat, jumped onboard and dragged the net ashore without breaking the net. Peter gave the man several large fish, then sat by the fire and watched him cook. No one dared ask the man who he was. We all knew he was Jesus.

When the meal was prepared, Jesus said, "Come and have breakfast." Jesus broke the bread and gave it to us, then he did the same with the fish. This was the third time Jesus appeared to us after he defeated death.

When we finished eating, Jesus said to Simon Peter and then to me, "Come with me."

As we walked the shoreline along the Sea of Tiberias, Jesus asked Peter, "Simon Peter, do you love me more than these men love me?" Peter had waited since the night at the high priest's courtyard to speak to Jesus.

He said, "Yes, Lord, you know that I love you."

Jesus looked at Peter and said, "I want you to teach my new believers."

Then Jesus asked Peter again, "Simon, do you truly love me?"

Peter was afraid Jesus doubted his love. He answered Jesus with emotion and said, "Yes, Lord, you know I love you."

Jesus slowed down his pace then and said to Peter, "Simon Peter, I want you to take care of my new church."

After he spoke these words, Jesus stopped and asked Peter the same question, "Do you love me?"

Peter was hurt as Jesus had asked this question for the third time. He looked deep into Jesus' eyes and answered him, saying, "Lord, you know all things, you know I love you."

Jesus nodded his head in agreement, then he said, "Peter, I want you to guide my new church.

"When you were young, you made your own decisions and you went your own way. Now you must follow me. I tell you the truth, when you are old, your ministry will end with your crucifixion."

Peter and Jesus discussed many matters that morning as we walked the shoreline. When we turned around to come back to our friends, Peter asked Jesus about me. He said, "What about him?"

Jesus answered Peter and said, "If I want John to remain alive until I return, what is that to you? You must follow me to the cross."

Jesus stopped with Peter and me along the shoreline. We all turned toward the sea and watched the waves roll to our feet. Jesus reached down after a time, picked up a stone, tossed it into the water, then he said to us, "I love you with the same love I love my Father. My love will always remain with you and your joy will be complete if you love each other as I love you. Men, feed my lambs and guide my sheep." Jesus left us then to return to our friends by ourselves.

"I do not know him," are five words Peter never forgot. Peter failed Jesus when Jesus was on trial for his life. Peter denied knowing Jesus once, twice, and three times before the rooster crowed to announce another morning sunrise. Jesus turned toward Peter then and made direct eye contact. Peter was a strong man. He couldn't hold Jesus' gaze. His spirit broke, and he left John in the courtyard by himself to support Jesus.

Peter left and wept bitterly, but he didn't return to his successful fishing business. As he shuffled along the dusty road to his lodging, Peter remembered a day in Capernaum. Jesus preached and the people departed from him because his words were too hard to accept. When the crowd vacated the synagogue that morning, Jesus looked around the empty room and said to the twelve disciples, "Don't you want to leave me?"

As Peter walked away from the high priest's courtyard the night he denied Jesus, he remembered stepping forward to speak for the group at the Capernaum synagogue. He put his arm around Jesus' shoulder and said, "Lord, where else can we go? You have the words of eternal life; and we believe you are the Christ, the Son of the living God."

Peter demonstrated the depth of his love for Jesus when he stood with Jesus after everyone else walked away.

On this darkest of dark nights, Peter made a mistake, but the words he spoke at Capernaum about Jesus remained Peter's truth.

Jesus had significant plans for Simon Peter's life. Jesus shared those plans with Peter and John the morning they went for a walk after breakfast.

Jesus was an evangelist who came from Heaven to minister to religious people for three years. He managed an organization consisting of twelve men and an assortment of other followers who came in and out of his ministry. His primary job function was to travel and preach, teach, and perform miraculous signs through the Father who was in him.

Jesus knew when he sent the Holy Spirit to his disciples on the Day of Pentecost, this miracle would add meaningful new ministry challenges. Jesus asked Peter to lead the believers in a new role when he ascended to Heaven. He asked Peter to teach the new believers who were still to come, to instruct the mature believers who were already here, and to pastor an enduring church that was yet to be built. It would be an extended church filled with new believers that would reach far beyond the Jewish borders.

This was an enormous responsibility for anyone, especially a plain-spoken fisherman from Galilee who was surrounded by ten men of similar background and education. Jesus had only one concern. He asked Peter once, twice, and three times, "Do you love me?"

Why was the love condition so important to Jesus?

True love never quits. The ones who truly love, invest their lives in the ones they love. They give their all to keep their loved ones safe and whole.

When Jesus walked with Peter and John that morning, He asked Peter to change from a hired hand to a shepherd and to lead a public ministry that would quickly supersede his own public ministry.

Jesus loved his Father. He followed Him and did what He asked. His love for his Father sustained Jesus throughout his time with the disciples, especially the last day. Jesus asked Peter to follow him all the way to his own cross.

The Holy Spirit would gift Peter with resources needed to achieve Jesus' goals. His love for Jesus would sustain him to the end.

He Ascended to Heaven

Acts 1:1-14

Jesus conquered death. He appeared to us over a forty-day period. He taught us many things pertaining to the Kingdom of God.

As his time on earth came to an end, Jesus walked with us to the Mount of Olives. When we were seated at our familiar place on the hill, one of the disciples asked Jesus, "Lord, has the time come for you to restore the kingdom to Israel?"

Jesus answered the disciple and said, "The Father has authority over time and seasons. This is something we may not know until it happens. You should be prepared to receive the Father at any time."

Jesus was excited and sad at the same time. He spent thirty-three years on earth and now he was going home. He stood before us and said, "My time with you has come to an end. You will not see me again until your time here ends.

"Listen to me closely. Do not leave Jerusalem. Wait here for the gift the Father promised you. John the Baptist baptized with water, but in a few days, you will be baptized with the Holy Spirit. You will receive miraculous power when the Holy Spirit comes on you, and you will be witnesses for me in Jerusalem, and in all Judea, Samaria, and to the ends of the earth."

When the Messiah finished delivering his final instructions to us, he came to each disciple and shared a kind word of encouragement and a loving touch. Then he relaxed for a moment and said to everyone, "My friends, we had fun, didn't we? Thank you for your faithfulness. I love you with the love of my Father. Love each other as I love you."

As the Son of God finished speaking to us, he left the ground and ascended toward Heaven before our eyes. We lost sight of Jesus when a cloud hid him from our view. As we stared intently toward Heaven, hoping for one last glance of Jesus, two men dressed in white suddenly stood beside us.

They said, "Men of Galilee, why do you stare toward the sky. The Son of God is in Heaven. A day will come when this same Jesus comes back in the same way you have seen him go to Heaven."

We shared a common life with Jesus Christ for three years. He was our leader, and he was our friend. He provided everything we needed and now he was gone for good.

There was a permanent sense of loss within the group. We would never see Jesus again in this lifetime.

We were finally alone. What should we do? How should we act? We were eleven men who had to make a hard choice for ourselves. Should we walk away on our own to live a settled life based on our own merit? Or should we band together with faith, return to Jerusalem to wait for the Holy Spirit, and live a new life with the Spirit of Life.

We walked back to Jerusalem together. We were eleven individuals, but we chose to face the city that brutally killed Jesus as one.

When we arrived, we went to the upper room we rented and locked the door. Fresh baked bread and cooked fish smells filled our living quarters. The women had worked to prepare the midday meal while we were gone.

Everyone stopped their activities. They gathered around us and waited for Peter to speak. Peter smiled a big grin, then said, "It's been an amazing morning. I still don't trust my eyes. We watched the Messiah ascend to Heaven from the Mount of Olives. Before Jesus left, he told us to wait in Jerusalem to receive the baptism of the Holy Spirit."

Everyone's eyes riveted to Peter. Each man and woman received this news as a factual statement. No one left us to walk away from this truth. We started a new life at that moment. Our hearts filled with a mixture of excitement, sadness, and fear. We joined together in like mind to wait for the Spirit of Life. The disciples, the women, Jesus' mother Mary and Jesus' brothers bonded as one to wait in constant prayer.

Can you imagine what the Word of Life felt and thought as he watched creation come into being? Can you visualize what Mary and Martha felt and thought as Jesus called to Lazarus and watched their brother walk away from his entombment?

Jesus walked with the disciples for forty days after he left the tomb, teaching those closest to him about the Kingdom of God. Can you envision what it was like to be with the risen savior and share in those special moments?

I can only imagine watching as Jesus ascended from earth. Think about it. He left the ground, disappeared into the clouds, and returned to Heaven to sit at His Father's right hand.

Wait on Spirit. We leave nothing to the imagination when we worship the living God who actively participates in our daily life through the Holy Spirit.

A Child Is Born

Luke 1:1-2:7

Bright sunlight spilled through the upper room's open windows. The light contributed to everyone's high spirits as we talked about Jesus' ascension and prepared the table for our midday meal. When we all settled at our places, I blessed the food, then handed Peter a loaf of bread.

Peter broke the loaf in half and said, "This bread symbolizes the body of our risen savior, Jesus Christ. Eat this in remembrance of the life he lived before the people and us. May we live the same life when we are baptized by the Holy Spirit and walk with the Spirit of Life."

When we finished eating the bread, I passed Peter the wine pitcher. He filled a cup and said, "This wine symbolizes the blood of Christ spilled for us. Jesus set aside his life to give everyone a new path to salvation and entry to the Kingdom of God. As you drink from this cup, remember how he showed his love for you and me. What more can we do than set aside our old life and love each other as Jesus loved his Father?"

After the cup was passed around the table, we sang a hymn, then enjoyed our meal.

Mary, Jesus' mother, spoke up as we lounged around the table sharing a light conversation. She cast her eyes around the room and said with a friendly smile, "Now is the time to tell you a story that has yet to be told. My husband Joseph is not the biological father of our son, Jesus."

Everyone in the room sat up and gave their full attention to Mary as she finished this revealing sentence. Her smile broadened as she observed the looks on the faces of her family and friends. She continued with her story and said, "Joseph and I lived in Nazareth. I was a young virgin when we pledged to be married. We loved each other deeply and spent every moment together we could. As is the Jewish custom, I was Joseph's wife, and he was my husband during our betrothal period. My husband lived in his parent's home and I lived in my family's home while we waited for our marriage to be consummated on our wedding night.

"One day as I shopped in the open market, a handsome man in an elegant white robe appeared to me and said, 'Greetings Mary, I am the angel Gabriel. God has sent me to tell you, you are highly regarded in Heaven. The Lord is with you!'

"As you can imagine, I was greatly troubled by Gabriel's words. What could this greeting possibly mean for me, a simple girl from Galilee? I was bewildered and fearful as the angel placed his hand on my elbow and gently guided me to a quiet place to talk.

"When we reached the outskirts of the marketplace, Gabriel turned to me and said, 'Mary, do not be afraid. God is with you and He will not leave you. You are a lucky woman. God has chosen you above all others to give birth to His son, and you shall name him Jesus. You and Joseph shall raise God's son as your own until Jesus' time comes to reveal himself to the world. When his Father calls Jesus forward, he will be great and will be called Son of the Most High.'

"I was stunned by Gabriel's words. My face flushed and my heart pounded through my chest as I tried to catch my breath. Why pick me? What would this mean for my life? I was Joseph's wife. Would Joseph believe me when I told him I carried God's child? How could anyone believe I carried God's child?

"My mind spiraled with these thoughts until my spirit finally settled my soul. 'How will this be, Gabriel? You know I am a virgin,' I asked as I looked into the angel's eyes."

The angel smiled with confidence and said, "If God can bring the heavens and earth into being, Mary, He can create His child in you. The holy one to be born will be called Son of God. Mary, the Heavenly Father is preparing to move in a mighty way before the children of Israel. Nothing is impossible with God. Even Elizabeth your relative is with child in her old age. She, who was barren at an old age, is six months pregnant. The child she carries will be filled with the Holy Spirit at birth. He will grow to manhood and speak for God with the power of Elijah. His words will prepare the people to meet the Son of God."

"My confidence rose as Gabriel spoke to me and God's presence manifest itself in me. I closed my eyes and spoke directly to 'I AM.' I said, 'I am your servant, Lord. I trust you with my life. I will gladly mother your Child and nurture him all the days of his life. May it be to me as you have said.' When I finished speaking to God, Gabriel left me as he came.

"Night came early, and I retired to my room holding the angel's words close to my heart. Before new daylight began to filter through the dark night, the Holy Spirit filled my room, and the power of the Most High overshadowed me. My senses were overwhelmed with light and warmth and love. I don't know how it happened, but I was pregnant with God's Child. I whispered to 'I AM' and said, 'I love you, Lord. The Child you have created for me to bear will be great. His name will be Jesus and he will be called Son of the Most High.'

"When morning arrived, I dressed and scurried off to Joseph's home to help with the family breakfast. I was not ready to tell Joseph about God's plan for our life, but I did share with him about Elizabeth. He was excited to hear she was with child and agreed I should go to her and assist with the birth. I hurried to get ready. After Joseph loaded my father's donkey, I set out for Zechariah and Elizabeth's home in the hill country of Judea.

"When I arrived at their home and secured the donkey, I called out to Elizabeth and waited on the front porch. Elizabeth came running to me. She was filled with the Holy Spirit and exclaimed to me in a loud voice, 'Mary, feel my baby. When my ears heard your greeting, the child in my womb leaped for joy. Why am I so blessed that you have come to me?'

"I grabbed her arm and we walked to the kitchen table where we sat and held hands. I answered her and said, 'The angel Gabriel told me you and Zechariah were with child.' I told her every word the angel shared with me and then announced to her that I was pregnant with the Heavenly Father's Son.

"Elizabeth stood up and came to me. She held me in her arms and looked me in my eyes and said, 'Mary, blessed are you for believing what the Lord has said will be accomplished. Blessed are you among women and blessed is the child you will bear.'

"I stayed with Elizabeth about three months. I left after she gave birth to a son who Zechariah named John. You know him as John the Baptist. The child lost his parents at an early age, so he lived in the desert where he grew and became strong in spirit. His clothes were made of camel hair and he wore a leather belt around his waist. His food was locusts and wild honey. John the Baptist was about 30 years old when he appeared publicly to Israel preaching and announcing the coming of the Messiah.

"I was worried as I started my journey back to Nazareth. I could barely hide the fact I was pregnant. Joseph would know I was with child when he looked into my eyes and hugged me.

"I loved my husband more that day than the day I left to stay with Elizabeth and Zechariah. Would Joseph accept the good news I was pregnant with God's child or put me away quietly? He could legally divorce me publicly or worse.

"As these thoughts sifted through my heart, mile after mile, I remembered Elizabeth's words, 'Mary, blessed are you for believing what the Lord has said will be accomplished. Blessed are you among women and blessed is the child you will bear.' These words encouraged me, but they didn't stop me from fretting over the confrontation I knew was coming when I got home.

"As tears pooled in my eyes and spilled down my cheeks, the angel Gabriel appeared before me. He put his arm around me and said, 'Mary, cheer up. Place your faith in the Heavenly Father and your husband, Joseph. Joseph is a righteous man with a heart for you and for God. Be patient with Joseph. He will not abandon you or the child that you bear. You and Joseph shall raise God's son as your own until his Heavenly Father calls Jesus forward.'

"When Joseph saw me approach his home, he ran across the front yard to the street to greet me. He picked me up, swung me around and kissed me when he set me down. It was the best welcome a wife could hope from her husband.

"I grabbed Joseph's hand and guided him to chairs sitting on the front porch, where we sat together and shared in small talk about my stay with Elizabeth and the journey home.

"God was with me. When I gathered the courage to speak with Joseph in earnest, I said, 'Joseph, I have something life-changing I must share with you. I don't expect you to understand immediately, but I hope you will have confidence in my love for you, and you will listen and take my words to the Lord before you react.'

"Joseph let my hand go and sat back in his chair. He looked me in the eyes with a concerned expression and said, 'Of course, Mary. Do not be troubled. Tell me what's on your heart.'

"I smiled at my husband and told him everything I knew about God's miraculous intervention in Zechariah's and Elizabeth's life, and the mighty works God planned for their child. Joseph returned my smile and said, 'Mary, that is great news. If Elizabeth's words are true, God is at work in Israel and the Messiah is coming! What makes this life-changing for you and me?'

"I reached across to hold Joseph's hand and said, 'Joseph, I am three months pregnant with God's child.' Joseph was shocked as he absorbed these words. He pulled away from me as deep sadness consumed his spirit. He spoke softly, but I could feel the anger, sadness and confusion in his voice as he said, 'No, Mary. That's not possible. Tell me the truth. How did this pregnancy come to be?'

"I sat still for a time gathering my composure. God was with me, but it didn't soften the blow Joseph's words delivered to my heart. I forced myself to smile and reflect the sweet countenance of the Holy Spirit in me. I shared every word the angel Gabriel gave me then told Joseph how the Holy Spirit overshadowed me and created the Son of God in my womb. Joseph listened intently to every word I spoke, but he did not believe me.

"He thought for a few minutes in silence, then he said, 'Mary, your story is pure fantasy. I love you with all my heart. I will always love you. And I wish the best for you and your child, but I will not father another man's child. We are finished. Don't worry, I will divorce you quietly, so you aren't exposed to public disgrace.'

"I stood to leave without speaking another word. I had shared the words God gave me, and Joseph had spoken. The tears flowed freely from my heart to my eyes and down my cheeks as I stepped down the front porch steps. When my feet touched the ground, I turned and smiled at Joseph then began the lonely walk home.

"At that moment, the Holy Spirit spoke to me as if He were standing next to me. He said, 'Mary, do not be afraid. Nothing is impossible with God.'

"Joseph stayed in a bad mood for days. He kept my secret in his heart as he struggled with his decision to divorce me. Joseph loved me deeply. What if my words were truth? Could he live with his mistake?

"An angel of the Lord finally appeared to Joseph in a dream and said, 'Joseph, do not be afraid to take Mary home as your wife. What is conceived in her is from the Holy Spirit. Mary is a virgin, and she will give birth to a son. Joseph, you will name the child, Jesus. God has come to the world, Joseph, and he will save his people from their sins.'

"Joseph woke with a start when the angel of the Lord departed. He shook his head and smiled at this fabulous news until the enormity of the circumstance overwhelmed him. He was the earthly father of the Son of God. He slipped from his bed and fell to his knees and prayed. He praised God for this mighty challenge with a spirit of thanksgiving. Then he asked the Lord for all the gifts he would need to raise his family with all God's blessings.

"The Holy Spirit came upon Joseph early that morning and stayed with him all the days of his life. My husband was a righteous man who cherished me and raised all our children with the love and wisdom and strength of God.

"Joseph rose from prayer at daybreak and dressed. He came for me when the sun sat in the morning sky and took me home to be his wife. We completed our marriage vows the same day.

"In those days, the government issued a decree that said a census should be taken throughout the entire Roman world. Everyone was required to travel to their hometown to register. Joseph and I belong to the house and line of David, so we went from Nazareth to Bethlehem, the city of David. The trip was memorable for me. Try riding a donkey when you're nine months pregnant. I was ready to lay down and rest when we arrived in the town, but all the rooms in the inns were filled. My contractions started by the time Joseph finally negotiated a space for us in a barn attached to an inn. The innkeeper's wife hurried to me. She made me comfortable in our makeshift dwelling. After several hours of labor, we delivered a beautiful son Joseph named, Jesus.

"God's light and love filled the barn as angels rejoiced with Joseph and me at the birth of God's son. They sang out with pure notes, 'Immanuel, the Holy One. God is with us. Praise be to the Father in Heaven who loves His children and keeps His word. The Messiah has arrived. Praise be to the Father. We worship a living and loving God. A Savior has been born who has come to save the world from sin.'

"When the angels faded into the background, Joseph and I cleaned our child, then I nursed Jesus until he fell asleep. I slept while Jesus slept. Joseph took Jesus from my arms, wrapped his son in cloths and placed him in a manger so he could rest after the long day's journey.

"Before he called it a day, Joseph stepped outside to look toward the heavens. He was amazed to see magnificent stars standing watch over the city."

God's Son was born in humble circumstance to faithful parents. We can all rejoice. His name is Immanuel, which means, "God is with us."

A Savior Is Born

Luke 2:8-40, Matt 2:1-23

Mary paused for a moment to gather her thoughts. She smiled with pure joy as she began sharing with us again. She said, "Early that morning, shepherds reverently approached us. They fell to their knees and worshiped our baby who lay in the manger. The spokesman for these men said to me, 'We are shepherds who live in the fields nearby. Last night we were tending our flocks. We were terrified when the glory of the Lord suddenly shone all around us. An angel of the Lord told us, "Do not be afraid. I bring you good news of great joy that is for all people. Today in the town of David a Savior has been born to you. He is Christ the Lord. Go to Bethlehem and share these words with the child's parents. This will be the sign for you: You will find the baby wrapped in cloth lying in a manger." When the angel finished speaking to us, the sky filled with angels praising God and saying, 'Glory to God in the highest, and on earth peace to men whom His favor rests.'

"The angel's message about Jesus was not lost on the shepherds. They left their fields to worship the Christ child. They spread the good news of great joy they heard and saw with their circle of life in Bethlehem. When they finished, the shepherds returned to their fields glorifying and praising God.

"I imagine each time they looked toward the star canopy that covered their fields, the shepherds recalled the company of angels sing, 'Glory to God in the highest, and on earth peace to men on whom His favor rests.' Each year, they must have wondered with anticipation when the Savior, who is Christ the Lord, would begin his reign on earth.

"As you know, Jewish law has many customs related to circumcision, purification, and consecration that are spread out over time. Since the temple in Jerusalem is five miles from Bethlehem, Joseph found work as a carpenter and rented us a house in Bethlehem.

"When the day came to fulfill the law of the Lord related to first born males, Joseph and I took Jesus to the temple in Jerusalem. A man named Simeon, who was filled with the Holy Spirit, met us in the temple courts. He stretched out his arms before me and asked to hold Jesus. I glanced toward Joseph, who nodded yes, and I gently placed our son into this man's arms.

"Jesus bonded with Simeon's heart as he quietly rested against the man's chest. Simeon closed his eyes in prayer, then he looked up to us with a vibrant smile and spoke for all in the temple court to hear. He said, 'God promised me I would not die until I saw the Lord's Christ.' Lifting Jesus up above his head for all to see, Simeon praised God and said, 'Sovereign Lord, as you have promised, I am now freed from this life in peace. I have seen with my own eyes Your salvation which You have prepared in the sight of all people, a light for revelation to the world and glory for your people Israel.'

"Joseph and I marveled at the words Simeon spoke. He blessed us as he handed Jesus back to me, then he spoke directly to me and said, 'Mary, this child is destined to be the Savior for many and the stumbling block for many more in Israel. Those who love Jesus will love the Father and those who don't love Jesus will not love the Father because they do not know God. This is a great day to celebrate, but you should be prepared. You and your son will suffer great anguish in this lifetime.' Simeon left us to our thoughts and walked away into the crowd when he finished speaking his words."

Mary stopped her narrative and asked for a drink to quench her thirst. I rose from my seat and filled her cup with wine. When she was satisfied, she began her story again and said, "We left the temple at dusk and traveled back to Bethlehem in the dark. A bright star assisted the moon illuminate the dusty road from Jerusalem to Bethlehem.

"Three Magi from the east waited for us in the courtyard when we arrived at home. The men bowed before us as we approached them. They called our small child, King of the Jews, when they saw him. Then they bowed lower and worshiped Jesus as their Lord before they opened their treasures and presented him with gifts of gold, incense, and myrrh.

"Joseph and I were humbled by their humility and generosity as we stood with our son before these wise men. Joseph eventually addressed the Magi and said, 'It is late in the evening. We are all hungry. Join us in our home and share our meal. We hope you will tell us the story of your journey.'

"I nursed Jesus in a back room while Joseph prepared a simple meal, and the Magi made themselves comfortable in our home.

"The wise men sipped the wine Joseph served and began their story. The elder among them said, 'We are astrologers from the east. God came to us in a dream and told us to search for His star in our sky. God said the star would be the sign the Messiah, The King of the Jews, was born. He told us the child would be called Immanuel; God is with us. We were overjoyed when the Messiah's star appeared in our eastern sky. We gathered ourselves and prepared to journey to Jerusalem to worship God's child. We traveled straight to King Herod's court and told him this story when we arrived in the Jewish capital city. We assumed the king would also rejoice at this news and know where the child was located. Quite the opposite. Herod was deeply disturbed and all of Jerusalem with him. We learned later; the king was a ruthless man. Herod called together the chief priests and the teachers of the law and asked them where the Christ was to be born. They told him, Bethlehem in Judea. When he learned where to look for the infant, he removed everyone from his presence. He wanted to know the child's age, so he asked us the date we first saw the star. We told him the exact time, then he sent us to Bethlehem to search for the child.

"'The Messiah's star appeared to us again when we left the king's palace. We followed the star directly to your home. We want you to know we believe your child is in danger. We are supposed to report directly to Herod when we find Jesus so he can come and worship him. The look in Herod's eyes was unmistakable. He will not come to worship the Christ child. God has told us to avoid Herod when we return to our homeland. We plan to follow God's instruction and take a different route when we leave tonight.'

"The wise men finished their meal with us, worshipped Jesus who laid in the manger, then quickly moved to the courtyard. The Messiah's star was gone when I looked to the sky. I watched the Magi mount their camels then ride into the dark and disappear from our lives forever.

"When the courtyard settled back to its normal night sounds, I glanced toward Joseph and said, 'Joseph, is our baby in danger?'

"Joseph shrugged his shoulders and said, 'I don't know, Mary. God's angels watch over us. God will protect us. Besides, what can we do now? Let's clean the kitchen and go to bed.'

"That night an angel came to Joseph in his dreams and said, 'Joseph, get up! Take the child and his mother and escape to Egypt. Stay there until I tell you because Herod is going to search for the child and will kill him.'

"Joseph woke me and told me his dream. We rose together, packed our belongings, and escaped to Egypt that night.

"When Herod realized he had been outwitted by the Magi, he committed a great atrocity. He gave orders to kill all the boys in Bethlehem who were two years old and under.

"We stayed in Egypt for some time. Joseph and I tried our best to live a normal life in a foreign land. After Herod died, an angel came to Joseph in his dreams and said, 'Joseph, get up. Take the child and his mother and return to the land of Israel. The ones who tried to kill the child are dead.'

"Joseph obeyed God and promptly took us to Israel. We eventually made our way to Galilee where we made our home in Nazareth. Joseph returned to his carpentry business and Jesus grew and became strong. He was an extraordinary child; filled with wisdom and the grace of God."

Life rarely plays out as we plan. Joseph was a faithful and obedient man. He and Mary created a home for their son wherever they lived in whatever circumstance they faced. Joseph knew to listen for God's voice, then promptly obey Spirit's words to protect his wife and child and provide for his family.

As God's children, we walk in Spirit's light. We live a common life with Jesus Christ when we are faithful and obedient to Spirit's voice, wherever we are and in whatever circumstances we face.

Age Twelve

Luke 2:41-52

"Every year we took Jesus to Jerusalem to the Feast of the Passover with our family and friends. When Jesus was twelve years old, we all went to Jerusalem. This was our tradition. After the feast was over, Joseph and I began the journey home. We assumed Jesus was traveling with his friends in our group. We had no idea he had remained behind in the temple courts, sitting with the teachers of the law, listening to their lessons and asking them questions.

"We traveled a full day before we realized Jesus was missing. We frantically searched for our son in our group of people before we returned to Jerusalem. We scoured the city before we found Jesus in the temple courts on the third day.

"We were amazed to see the large crowd gathered around our son and the teachers. Everyone who heard him was impressed by his understanding and his answers. Joseph and I marched through the crowd to our son. Joseph lifted Jesus from his seat on the ground by his arm.

"I looked my son in the eyes with a strong parent's gaze and said, 'Son, why have you treated us like this? Your father and I have anxiously searched for you.'

"Jesus returned my gaze with loving eyes of a respectful child and said, 'Mother, why have you searched for me. Didn't you know I had to be in my Father's house?'

"Joseph and I looked at each other in disbelief. We were not aware our son already knew his unique relationship with his Father in Heaven. We did not respond to Jesus at the time.

"Joseph reached down and placed his hand in Jesus' hand, then he said to the teachers, 'Thank you for caring for our child. We apologize for interrupting your lesson.'

"A younger teacher of the law named Nicodemus stood up and came to where we stood as a family. He shook Joseph's hand and hugged Jesus, and said, 'The gift was ours. Your son is remarkably blessed with wisdom from God. We hope you will bring him to us often to discuss the scriptures.'

"Joseph smiled at Nicodemus but didn't make a commitment. We walked out of the temple courtyard as a family and began the journey back to Nazareth. Jesus filled our ears with everything he learned during his time with the teachers. Joseph and I listened closely, praising God we were chosen to raise this magnificent child.

"Peter, Jesus grew up before us with wisdom and stature, and in favor with God and men. I have treasured up all these memories and have pondered them in my heart for myself until today. Today I share them with you all to make my joy complete.

"My Son has returned to his Father in Heaven from which he came. I will not see my boy again until I pass from this life to the next. I will miss him terribly, but his task here is complete."

Mary's children and the other women came to comfort her then as she began to shed tears of joy mixed with deep sadness.

I stood and came to Mary and said, "Mary, blessed are you for believing what the Lord said would be accomplished. Blessed are you among women for raising this child to become a man before men, Christ our Lord."

We make choices throughout life. The easy decision may not be God's choice for us. Wait on God. Listen for Spirit's voice and He will show us His way.

Mary chose the hard way, and she birthed a child who became a man before men, Christ our Lord.

A New Apostle

Acts 1:15-26

Judas Iscariot was the twelfth disciple. He walked away from us at our last supper with Jesus, and Satan took him for his own. Judas guided those who arrested our Lord. The shame Judas carried broke him. He died at his own hand during our darkest days. The Jewish priests took the money Judas earned for his transgression and bought the field where he died. Everyone in Jerusalem called the place, 'The Field of Blood' because of the grisly results of his suicide.

Peter led the small gathering of believers who waited in Jerusalem for the Holy Spirit baptism. The group numbered about one hundred twenty men and several women. Some of these people faithfully walked with the eleven disciples from Jesus' baptism through his resurrection.

Peter studied the scriptures and discerned another leader was needed to replace Judas. He stood before the small congregation and said, "King David wrote about Judas in the scriptures. He tells us, 'Let another take his place in leadership.' Therefore, we need to choose one who has been with us the whole time Jesus walked with us, from the time he was baptized to the time Jesus was taken up from us. This is important because the new apostle will be a witness with us of Jesus Christ's resurrection."

The congregation gathered together and proposed two names; Barsabbas and Matthias. Then they prayed, "Lord, you know everyone's heart. Show us which one of these two you have chosen to take over Judas' apostolic ministry."

When they finished the prayer, we cast lots. Matthias was chosen, so we added him to the eleven apostles.

One day Matthias was a follower. The next day he was a leader preparing to testify as a witness that Jesus Christ, the same man the religious people killed, rose from the dead and ascended to Heaven. Imagine the emotions he felt and the thoughts that raced through his mind. Was he ready? Could he handle this situation? Would he disappoint his family and friends, and fail his Messiah? These are all rational thoughts to contemplate when life changes dramatically.

Our Father knows us. He does not ask for more than we can give. Our trust in Him grows when we remain with and follow the Holy Spirit. Our confidence and faith grow when we understand our task and realize God doesn't intend for us to do His work for Him.

Our trouble begins when we get ahead of the Holy Spirit and we attempt to do God's job.

When we wait with the Lord, our Father gives us what we need to live before others His way at the time of His choosing.

Matthias and the others patiently waited in Jerusalem for the Holy Spirit baptism.

The Holy Spirit Arrives

Acts 2:1-13

The congregation of believers assembled in one place on the morning of Pentecost. We were patiently waiting on the Lord to fulfill his promise to us when the sound of wind suddenly came toward us, like a locomotive train from Heaven. The noise consumed the whole house where we sat. The believers rejoiced with Peter and me in awe-filled respect when we saw what appeared to be tongues of fire separate and rest upon each of us. Each person's spirit was united with the Holy Spirit and we began to speak in languages we did not understand.

The congregation of believers unlocked the doors and spilled from the house onto the street to celebrate with the Holy Spirit. We no longer feared the religious elite.

As I watched my friends delight in God's gift, I remembered the words Jesus spoke to us at the Mount of Olives: "I love you as I love my Father. You must believe me it is in your best interest that I go away now. Spirit cannot come to you until I send him. When He comes to you, He will show the world its guilt regarding sin, righteousness, and judgement.

"Now is the time for grief, my friends. You will weep and mourn for a short time while the world rejoices at my death. You grieve now, but believe me as I say to you, do not lose heart. Your grief will turn to joy. You will see me again and no one will take away your joy. On that day, you will no longer need to ask me for anything. You can ask the Father in my name and you will receive what you request. On that day, your joy will be complete."

My joy was complete as I danced in the street with the others, speaking a language I did not understand. Jesus kept his word. He ascended to Heaven and poured the Holy Spirit upon us!

Jerusalem was populated with God-fearing Jews from every nation under Heaven. When they heard the noise coming from our house, a crowd came together and formed around the apostles and our followers. Our visitors were confused because each one heard a believer speak their own language.

Struck with wonder, they asked each other, "Aren't these men Galileans? How is it we all hear them declare the wonders of God in our native language? What does this mean?"

Of course, some in the crowd made fun of us. The mockers said, "These people are drunk. They have had too much wine."

God was present, yet these people didn't believe the miracle. We shouldn't be surprised. God reveals Himself to everyone, and the world is still filled with unbelief.

A person has their reason why they don't believe in God. People view the evil that permeates the world today and say, "There is no God."

Other people experience personal tragedy and blame God. Their pain turns from grief to anger and then hate. They walk away from a living and loving Father for good because they are unwilling to accept that bad things happen to good people for reasons we do not understand in this lifetime.

Intellectuals reject God because they are unwilling to admit a higher being exists outside their limited scope of understanding of the universe and all that is created in it. They misunderstand or ignore the infinite gap between man's ability to think and make, and God's ability to create.

The Christian tradition is not passing forward like it has in past generations. What was valued by societies in the past is no longer valued by as many today. We see Christian churches empty as next generations walk away from their parents' and grandparents' religion.

The new world recognizes Jesus as a prophet or teacher, but fewer believe he is the Son of God. Godly power, love, and awe-filled respect is rarely associated with Jesus' name any longer. Consequently, Jesus is honored the same as other major religious teachers like Mohammed, Siddhartha Gautama Buddha, and Joseph Smith.

What are we missing today? The apostles were missing the Holy Spirit.

Ordinary people called to perform extraordinary work in Jesus' name sat in a house behind locked doors. When the Holy Spirit came to them with a sound like a locomotive train sent from Heaven, their new life began. They unlocked their doors, left their house, and went to the street. The congregation of believers' joy was complete as they danced in the street together, praising God and thanking Him for answering prayers in languages they did not understand when they woke that morning.

Jesus has kept his word. He has ascended to Heaven and pours the Holy Spirit upon those who believe in him!

The people from Jerusalem came to investigate the noise and were struck with wonder at the gifts the apostles and their followers displayed.

Changed Lives

Acts 2:14-47

The crowd outside our house quickly multiplied in size to thousands. We moved with the crowd to an open space with elevated ground to accommodate the people.

Peter was a plainspoken fisherman, not a public speaker. He always stood to the side with the other disciples and listened while John the Baptist and Jesus addressed crowds in these numbers.

I watched Peter struggle to profess his faith when three people challenged his loyalty to Jesus Christ in the chief priest's courtyard. Now he was called to address this crowd.

Simon Peter turned to me with butterflies in his stomach and the Holy Spirit in his spirit. He smiled and said, "John, are you ready to begin the ministry our Father has called us to live out in His Son's name?"

I returned my friend's smile, gave him a hug, and then said, "I am. Now step forward and deliver the words the Holy Spirit will give you in the name of our savior, Jesus Christ."

Peter stood with the apostles, raised his voice, and addressed the crowd. He said, "Listen carefully to what I have to say to you. These men are not drunk. It's nine o'clock in the morning! What you see and hear this morning, the prophet Joel foretold. He said, 'In the last days, God will pour out His Spirit on all people, and everyone who calls on the name of the Lord will be saved.'

"As you yourselves know, Jesus of Nazareth was a man accredited by God through the miracles, signs, and wonders God performed through him. This man was handed over to you for God's set purpose and with his foreknowledge. You killed him by nailing him to a cross with the help of evil men. It is impossible for death to keep its hold on him. God freed Jesus from the agony of death when He raised His Son from the dead. God has raised this

Jesus to life, and we are all witnesses of this fact. He is exalted now, sitting at the right hand of God. He has received the promised Holy Spirit from the Father and Jesus has poured out on us what you now see and hear.

"Therefore, let all Israel be assured of this: God has made this Jesus, whom you crucified, both Lord and Christ."

When the people heard Peter's words, they were cut to the heart. The people acknowledged they blindly followed their religious leaders and helped kill the Messiah, the Son of God. They called out to Peter and the other apostles and asked, "Brothers, what can we do to overcome this transgression?"

Peter spoke many words that morning. He warned, then pleaded with the people saying, "Save yourself from this corrupt generation. The promise of the Holy Spirit is for everyone the Lord our God will call. The promise is for you and your children, and for all who are far off. Repent and be baptized in the name of Jesus Christ for the forgiveness of your sins, every one of you, and you will receive the gift of the Holy Spirit."

Those who accepted his message were baptized, and about three thousand people were added to their number that day.

The crowd was filled with God-fearing Jews from every country in the known world. They kept the Jewish law. Their lifestyle reflected Jewish customs. They participated in Jewish rituals. And they patiently waited for the Messiah. Based on outward appearance, these people knew and loved the Father in Heaven.

When Jesus Christ came to these people, they should have recognized who he was and embraced him. What was going through their hearts and minds when they shouted to Pilate, "Crucify Jesus! Crucify Jesus! We want Barabbas," at the governor's palace?

These people feared man and loved their worldly lifestyle more than they loved God. They rejected the King of the Jews that day to save their way of life and their place in the synagogue. What was the consequence of their decision? They added their voice to a mob that sentenced the Son of God to death.

How did these people respond when the Spirit cut them to the heart with guilt for their part in killing the Son of God? Did they turn against the apostles like they turned against Jesus?

When Peter finished speaking that morning, three thousand people from the crowd yielded to the Holy Spirit and repented of their transgressions against God. The Godly men standing with Peter baptized them in the name of Jesus Christ and they received the gift of the Holy Spirit.

The Day of Pentecost miracle was not a onetime emotional experience that came and then faded into a pleasant memory from good times past. A movement began. Lives changed forever, and Christianity was born. Some of these people lost their lives. Others lost their positions in society, their homes, and their sources of income. Many sold their possessions and gave to anyone who had need.

As the days passed, all the believers devoted themselves to the apostles' teachings and fellowship, to the breaking of bread, and to prayer. They met together in temple courtyards every day. They broke bread together in their homes and ate together with glad and sincere hearts, praising God and enjoying the favor of all the people. Everyone was filled with awe as they shared everything in common. And each day, the Lord added new converts to the fellowship of believers.

We Do Not Have
Silver or Gold

Acts 3:1-26

One day, about three o'clock in the afternoon, Peter and I walked toward the temple to meet the congregation of believers. As we passed through the temple gate, called the "Beautiful Gate," I felt the Holy Spirit stir within me. When I turned to Peter, he simply nodded his head. He felt the same feeling.

I began to pray when we heard a beggar call to us. Peter and I looked straight at the man. He was a cripple, sitting on the ground, digging through his satchel.

Peter answered the man and said, "Look at us!" The crippled man set aside his bag and gave us his attention. I smiled as I thought to myself, *He expects us to give him money.*

Peter and I looked into the man's eyes, and Peter said, "We do not have silver or gold to give you. What we give is more precious. Our gift is given to you in the name of Jesus Christ: Walk!"

As these words passed Peter's lips, he reached down, grabbed the man's right hand, and helped him stand. The crippled man's feet and ankles instantly became strong.

The man was forty years old. He was overwhelmed with joy. He leaped and danced and praised God as he walked with us into the temple courts. All the people we saw recognized him as the crippled man who sat outside the Beautiful Gate. They were all filled with wonder at what happened to this man.

News of the healing quickly spread throughout the temple. People came running. All the people were astonished to see the healed man for themselves at a place called "Solomon's Colonnade."

The man held onto Peter and me as a large crowd formed around us. Peter began to speak as the crowd quieted to hear his words. He said, "Why does this miraculous sign surprise you? Why do you stare at John and me as if we performed this miracle with our own power or godliness? We didn't make this man walk. Our Father in Heaven has glorified His Son, Jesus Christ, this afternoon.

"You handed Jesus over to Pilate to be killed. You disowned him before Pilate, even though Pilate decided to let him go. You disowned the Holy and Righteous One and demanded a murderer be handed over in his place. You killed the author of life, but God raised Jesus from the dead. John and I are witnesses to all of this."

Peter paused for a moment and put his arm around the healed man's shoulders, then he said, "You all know this man. He was a forty-year-old cripple who could not walk. As you all can see, he is completely healed. He has been made strong by a faith that comes in the name of Jesus Christ."

Peter softened his voice then as he prepared to conclude his talk with this large gathering of religious people. The crowd moved closer to hear as Peter began to speak again. He said, "Now, brothers, I know you and your leaders acted in ignorance. When our Father raised His Son from the dead, He still chose to bless you by coming to you first to turn from your wicked way. Repent therefore and turn to God that your sins may be wiped away. Your life will change forever as you experience times of refreshing that come from the Lord."

Peter and John didn't speak in Jerusalem's streets to pagans that afternoon. The apostles spoke in God's temple at the time of prayer to devoted followers of the Jewish religion. These followers filled their minds with knowledge, and they kept busy with religious activity, yet Peter said, "I know you and your leaders acted in ignorance when you disowned the Holy and Righteous One and killed the author of life."

These people were dedicated to their religion. How could they be unaware or uninformed about the divine nature of Jesus Christ? They worshipped Jesus' Father. He performed miraculous signs and taught in the temple and the streets of Jerusalem for three years. If God was in them, they would have had awe-filled respect for the Father, and the Father would have pointed them to His Son.

Jesus told these people they did not know his Father. These people filled their life with religion, yet they did not worship the living God.

The people who stood before Peter at Solomon's Colonnade acted in ignorance when they followed their leaders and blindly handed Jesus over to Pilate to be killed. We act in ignorance when we fill our life with "religion" and set God aside to get through the day, the week, and our lifetime the best way we can.

Peter spoke God's words with love and kindness as he said, "When our Father raised His Son from the dead, He commanded us to bless you by coming to you first to turn each of you from your wicked way. Repent therefore and turn to God that your sins may be wiped away. It is time to live a new life that comes from the Lord."

Many remember a day when we gladly shared in the Holy Spirit's gifts in our daily life. Now our heads are filled with knowledge and special memories, and our lives are dominated by many activities we try to manage. At best, we feel close to God for a few minutes or an hour at church, during the special time we share with our children when we tuck them into bed, and those quiet moments in the car when we hear a meaningful praise song on the radio. We know to wait on the Lord and walk with the Spirit of life to live in His will in this dark world, but we just don't have time to wait. We do the best we can with what we have and hope we make good choices without Him.

God did not send His Son to start a new religion organized with rituals and activity. God sent us His Spirit to establish a spiritual relationship so we can share in a common life with Him. We are blessed that God loves us and still chooses to come to us when we have set Him aside.

Remember the times of refreshing that came from the Lord? Stress dissipates when we have a heart for God.

The Acts of Unschooled, Ordinary Men

Acts 4:1-22

The priests and Sadducees were angry that Peter and I taught the people Jesus rose from the dead. They came to the temple courtyard with the captain of the temple guard to arrest us. These men didn't hide their frustration as they pushed through the crowd to reach us. They bound our arms behind our backs like common criminals while we were still speaking to the people.

I had an overwhelming sense of calm. I remembered many of their faces from the night they bound my Lord at the olive grove. I looked to my friend, Peter, and expected him to be fighting mad. After all, he was a hot-tempered fisherman from Galilee. To my surprise, Peter was peaceful as he submitted to this shameful act performed by blind men who followed the will of hardened hearts. When the religious leaders finished arresting us, the soldiers seized us, marched us through the crowd, and threw us in jail for the night.

The Sadducees believed the new believers would scatter with changed hearts and minds if they disgraced us before the people. The opposite occurred. Many who heard God's words spoken that afternoon believed, and the number of men in the congregation of believers grew to about 5,000.

The next day, the jailers released Peter and me from prison and brought us before the high priest's court. The man who was formerly crippled, smiled and waved to us when we entered the court. We smiled back. Annas and Caiaphas were present, along with the other rulers, elders, and teachers of the law.

The chief prosecutor stood before the greatest minds of religious law and began to question us. He said, "It's my understanding, you two healed this crippled man by the temple gate called Beautiful. By what power or what name did you do this?"

I prayed as Peter stood to speak. As his eyes swept the room, Peter realized he addressed the body of decision makers who sentenced Jesus of Nazareth to death. He was not afraid. He was filled with the Holy Spirit.

He looked the prosecutor directly in the eyes and answered for all to hear. He said, "Rulers and elders of the people, if John and I are called to account for an act of kindness shown to a cripple and we are asked how he was healed, then know this, you and all the people of Israel. This man stands before you healed by faith in the name of Jesus Christ of Nazareth, the one you crucified, but God raised from the dead. Salvation doesn't come from anyone else because no other name is given under Heaven to men by which we must be saved."

The Sanhedrin was astonished by Peter's presentation and took note that we had been with Jesus. The religious scholars and politicians were surprised by our courage, and the fact we were unschooled, ordinary men. What could they say to us to dispute our experience and Peter's words? The Sanhedrin couldn't deny a godly action occurred. Everybody in Jerusalem knew we had performed an outstanding miracle, and all the people were praising God for what had happened.

I'm not sure which character flaw is worse: ignorance or arrogance? The Sanhedrin were foolish men who were shrouded in tradition, knowledge, and power. They joined together and agreed they could stop Peter and me from educating the people by commanding us to end our teaching ministry.

We stood before these decision makers with the crippled man by our side as Caiaphas rose from his seat to speak. He looked directly at Peter and me, and said, "Do not speak or teach at all in the name of Jesus."

The Holy Spirit washed over me as I heard these words.

I thought to myself as I looked to Peter, *No man can stop what God has chosen to complete through my life.*

When Caiaphas sat down, Peter addressed these strong words and said, "Judge for yourself whether it is right in God's sight to obey you rather than God. For we cannot help speaking about what we have seen and heard."

The Sanhedrin released us after they issued additional threats. What else could they do to punish us? All the people in Jerusalem were praising God for what had happened.

Annas and Caiaphas were present, along with the other rulers, elders, and teachers of the law. These were the men who pushed Pilate until he had Jesus crucified. They were the ones who had Pilate post guards at Jesus' tomb to prevent robbers from stealing the body. These were the men who spread the rumor throughout Jerusalem that in fact, the tomb was robbed, and Jesus didn't rise from the dead. These foolish men still fought God as they suffered with arrogance in ignorance.

The Holy Spirit had the final say with these men. God worked through the words and acts of these unschooled, ordinary men who were filled with the courage that comes when the Holy Spirit lives in us and with us.

God's truth separates us from the world. No man can stop what God has chosen to complete when we show up and act on our faith in the name of Jesus Christ.

Enable Us

Acts 4:23-31

Our friends were relieved when we returned to them, safe and sound. We all remembered the brutal treatment Jesus endured at the Sanhedrin's cruel hand. Peter and I shared what we experienced in the temple with the crippled man, and everything the chief priests and elders said to us.

Everyone was concerned when Peter said, "Caiaphas has commanded us to stop speaking or teaching in the name of Jesus."

Jesus' brutal torture at Caiaphas' feet was still fresh on everyone's mind.

Still, no one backed away. We all joined together as one voice and called out to God, praying, "Sovereign Lord, you created the heavens and the earth and the sea, and everything in them. Now Lord, we ask you to consider the Sanhedrin's threats and enable us, your servants, to speak your words with boldness. Stretch out Your hand to heal and perform miraculous signs and wonders through the name of your holy servant Jesus."

After we prayed, the Holy Spirit overwhelmed us. The place where we met shook. Everyone was filled with the Holy Spirit, and we spoke the word of God with boldness.

We don't need to be afraid, but certain situations like this deserve the respect fear garners. Jesus challenged the religious elite and the Sanhedrin had him beaten and killed with God's foreknowledge. Peter and John healed a cripple at the temple gate and the Sanhedrin had them arrested and thrown in jail. The religious elite were real adversaries who had shown they had no moral boundaries when they wanted to protect their position in society.

Our God is mighty. He is the alpha and the omega, the beginning and the end. He is the great "I AM." Our God created the heavens and the earth and the sea, and everything in them. The Creator is our Father. We are His children. No one can take us from our Father's grasp. If our Creator is for us, who can stand against God when the Holy Spirit lives in us and with us?

The congregation of believers committed their lives to this truth as they engaged in spiritual warfare. The apostles and believers did not fear the Sanhedrin, but they respected the evil power controlling them. They immediately came together in prayer. They did not pray to the Father for their safekeeping. They prayed for boldness to defy the Sanhedrin's command and glorify Jesus Christ through spoken words and miraculous signs and wonders.

God answered their prayers. Everyone was filled with the Holy Spirit and our Father enabled them all to speak the word of God with boldness.

Our circle of life includes people who enjoy a controlling position over us. Like the ruling elite Jesus, Peter and John confronted, these people may try to use their dominating influence to disrupt our lives while they protect their own power, position, and assets. These people often focus on reward and punishment to manipulate our behavior. Many fear the controlling ones because they can directly impact our personal lives in bad ways. For all intent and purpose, those who are afraid become slaves to the other person's will. Good people set God aside to follow another to protect their own power, position, relationships, or assets.

The apostles and believers did not fear the Sanhedrin, but they respected the evil power controlling the Sanhedrin. The congregation of believers were men and women full of faith and filled with the Holy Spirit. They understood they were engaged in spiritual warfare. They didn't focus on consequence or circumstance. They gave all their attention to God and went about their daily lives speaking truth with integrity in the open. And the Holy Spirit stood with them.

We have the same promise.

One in Heart and Mind

Acts 4:32-36, 5:1-16

I missed Jesus. I was with him every day, all day for three years. Although my life was rich in ministering to new believers and my spirit was filled with the Holy Spirit, it wasn't the same. I missed him.

One evening, I asked Peter to join me at the Mount of Olives. We prayed together, and my spirit lifted as we reminisced for hours into the night.

At one point I said, "Peter, I watched over Jesus the final night we shared this place with him. His last prayer was for his church. He was concerned about unity. Jesus lifted his voice to Heaven and said, 'Father, my prayer is for all those who will believe in me through the disciples' ongoing message. May they be one, as you and I are one. May they be in complete unity to show the world you sent me, and you love them as you love me.'"

Peter looked at me through the grey light of the night sky and shook his head in agreement. Then he said, "John, God is completing a mighty work within the congregation of believers. The Holy Spirit is alive in our midst. All the believers are one in heart and mind. I have never asked anyone for this, but no one claims their possessions for themselves. They share what they have with each other as needs arise. How many times has someone sold a building or land and brought us the proceeds to distribute as we've seen a need? Just the other day, Barnabas, the son of encouragement, sold a field he owned and brought us the money.

"The crowds in Jerusalem are blessed to witness the miracles and wonders we perform through God's power. We are blessed to witness daily miracles as uncommon people bond together and share in a common life through the name of Jesus Christ."

Among the new believers were a married couple, Ananias and his wife, Sapphira. They were swept up in the euphoric energy permeating some of the congregation of believers. They sold property they owned to give the proceeds to God without counting the cost.

Who knows Ananias' and Sapphira's actual motivation for giving? When they had their cash in hand, they asked each other, "What happens to us if hard times come and the church isn't able to take care of our needs?" The couple agreed they needed to hold back some money from the land sale. They discussed the amount they were willing to risk on God's blessings, and the amount they needed to withhold for tough times.

Ananias came to Peter and laid their gift at the apostle's feet. Peter thanked Ananias, then asked him this question: "Ananias, what amount of the land sale are you giving today?"

Ananias looked at Peter and said, "Sapphira and I decided to gift the full amount of the sale to the church."

Peter stared at the man for a while. His face was sad as he spoke his next words with a soft voice, "Ananias, how did Satan so fill your heart that you lied to the Holy Spirit? That land was your land before the sale. The proceeds were your cash after the sale. Any gift to God would have been appreciated. What made you think of doing such a thing? You haven't lied to me. You have lied to God."

When Ananias heard this, he collapsed and died. The facts surrounding Ananias' death quickly spread, and great fear seized everyone who heard what had happened.

Three hours later Sapphira came to Peter. She was not aware her husband died. Peter lifted the purse Ananias brought to him and asked, "Sapphira, tell me, is this the price you and Ananias got for the land?" Sapphira recognized the purse.

She smiled and said, "Of course, Peter. Yes, that is the price."

Peter shook his head in disbelief, then he said to her, "How could you agree to test the Spirit of the Lord? See the young men at the door? They just returned from burying your husband. They will carry you out and bury you beside him."

At that moment, she collapsed at Peter's feet and died.

Great fear seized the whole church and everyone else who heard about these events.

All the believers used to gather with us at Solomon's Colonnade. After Ananias' and Sapphira's deaths, everyone learned that God does not tolerate hypocrisy or deceit in His presence. People who had a different heart and mind from the congregation of believers did not dare join us. Nevertheless, many more men and women believed in the Lord and were added to our numbers.

Our reputation grew, and God was glorified through the many miraculous signs and wonders we performed. People brought the sick and laid them on mats in the street hoping Peter's shadow might fall on them when he walked by. People from towns surrounding Jerusalem also brought their sick and those tormented by evil spirits. All of them were healed. God was continually glorified through the mighty works completed through us and the congregation of believers.

Great fear seized the whole church as the people began to understand the spiritual warfare taking place in Jerusalem.

The death of Ananias and Sapphira was tragic. This married couple lived a comfortable life apart from God. Why join the congregation of believers, lie to God, and test the Spirit of the Lord?

Our Father blesses the believers who worship and serve Him with one mind and heart. God does not tolerate pretenders in His presence.

Jail Time

Acts 5:17-42

The high priest and his associates created unexpected problems for themselves when the Sadducees killed Jesus. Caiaphas was frustrated with his predicament and furious with all of us. He silenced Jesus to bring order back to temple life, and now we filled Jerusalem with Jesus' teaching and miraculous works of God.

Furthermore, Peter and I were determined to turn the people against him and his associates by convincing them Caiaphas was guilty of spilling Jesus' innocent blood. The high priest had to stop us before he lost control of Jerusalem and the temple. He called the captain of the temple guard forward and ordered the officer to throw all of us into the public jail.

Peter and I were teaching at Solomon's Colonnade with the other apostles when the soldiers broke through the crowd to arrest us. The Lord strengthened my heart as I looked toward Peter. He shrugged his shoulders and simply placed his hands behind his back to be bound for arrest by the soldier coming his way.

We spent the afternoon and evening in prayer, singing songs, and reminiscing about our life with Jesus. We eventually fell asleep sitting on the jail's cold, stone floor.

Sometime during the night, I felt a tap on my forehead and heard a voice say, "Wake up, John. It's time to leave this place."

An angel of the Lord stood before me. He opened the jail doors for us and brought us out of the building. When we all stood outside, the angel said, "Go, stand in the temple courts, and tell the people the full message of this new life."

At daybreak, we entered the temple courts and began to teach the people as we were told.

When Caiaphas arrived at work, he called to his clerk and said, "Notify the Sanhedrin we are meeting today. I want to speak with the full assembly of Israeli elders. Then summon the captain of the temple guard. Send him to the public jail to bring the apostles to me at the court."

A detachment of soldiers walked to the jail to secure us. As they entered the building, they noticed all the doors were locked, and jailers stood guard outside each jail cell. The jailer unlocked our jail cell and walked inside with the soldiers. They were shocked to find the room empty. The jailers all swore they did not sleep during the night as the soldiers unlocked every jail cell looking for us. The soldiers finished their search and concluded we disappeared during the night.

The officer in charge of the detachment reported his finding to the chief priests and his captain. Everyone was puzzled by our disappearance. They were afraid they faced another empty tomb when a priest came into Caiaphas' office and said, "Look! The men you put in jail yesterday are standing in the temple courts teaching."

The high priest shook with anger when he heard this news. He thought to himself, *These men are like their leader. They obey their God before others. Threatening language will not stop them.*

The captain didn't wait for an order. He and his officers left Caiaphas' office and went to the temple courts to arrest us again.

The captain feared the believers who surrounded us. He stopped his men before they entered the crowd and said, "Do not use force on these men. Their followers will stone us if we mistreat their leaders."

When the captain came to arrest us, we gathered quietly, and the officers brought us to the Sanhedrin to be questioned by the high priest.

Once again, we stood before the greatest religious minds and political leaders of the time. Caiaphas came forward and said to Peter and me, "We gave you strict orders not to teach in this name, and you fill Jerusalem with your words and works."

Peter and I said, "We must obey God rather than man!"

Then Peter stepped before us and said to the Sanhedrin, "The God of our fathers raised Jesus from the dead, the same Jesus you killed by hanging on a cross. God has exalted Jesus to His right hand that He might give forgiveness for the repentance of sins to Israel. We are all witnesses of these things, and so is the Holy Spirit, whom God gives to those who obey Him."

The Sanhedrin was furious with Peter when he finished speaking. The elders of Israel spoke over each other as they called out to the high priests, "These men must be put to death."

The Holy Spirit filled us with strength and confidence as we watched the Sanhedrin act out their anger toward us.

The elders settled down when a Pharisee named Gamaliel, who was honored by all people, stood before the Sanhedrin and had us removed from the assembly. He spoke with a clear voice to his peers, saying, "We must carefully consider what we intend to do with these men. Other leaders have appeared in our past who claimed to be somebody. Their followers dispersed once the leader was killed. Jesus' followers haven't scattered. They are growing in number by the day and their new leaders continue to perform signs and wonders that come from God. I advise you to leave these men alone. Let them go. If their purpose is of human origin, it will fail. But if it is of God, you will not be able to stop them. If we aren't careful, we will find ourselves fighting against God."

The Sanhedrin was persuaded by Gamaliel's reasoning. Caiaphas called us back to the assembly and had us beaten with a whip. Then he ordered us to stop speaking in the name of Jesus and let us go.

We left the Sanhedrin and rejoiced that we were counted worthy to suffer for the name of Jesus. Day after day, we returned to the temple and went from house to house teaching the good news that Jesus is the Christ.

God's chosen men suffered at the hands of the greatest religious minds and political leaders of their time. They were thrown in jail, threatened with death, and beaten with a whip because they filled Jerusalem with the words and works of Jesus Christ.

Did they quit when they faced adversity? Just the opposite, they rejoiced that they were counted worthy to suffer for the name of Jesus. The apostles preached the gospel before the Sanhedrin and returned to the temple courts and the streets of Jerusalem to tell the people the full message of their new life.

John and Peter and all the believers had a hard choice to make before the Sanhedrin—so do we now. Peter and John were in a fight for their life. They stood before the Sanhedrin without fear and answered the threat. They said, "We must obey God rather than man!"

As the dark world of unbelief closes in on our nation, the spiritual warfare surrounding us intensifies. Many are threatened to set aside what we know is right before God. We are led to believe we protect what we have if we change our ways to gain others favor. Do we bend to these people's will?

Seek God's truth with open eyes and a curious heart when we confront adversity. His truth will separate us from the darkness, and the Holy Spirit will show us a way to glorify our Father. Darkness will not be able to stop what God starts in us. Evil will find itself fighting against God.

A Man Full of Faith and the Holy Spirit

Acts 6:1-15, 7:1-60, 8:1-3

Stephen was a member of the congregation of believers. He was a man full of faith and the Holy Spirit. We all thought highly of Stephen. He was wise beyond his years, he had a servant's heart, and he did miraculous signs before the people.

Stephen enjoyed debating the good news of Jesus Christ with Synagogue of Freedmen members. Unfortunately, certain members of this synagogue were jealous of his intellect and opposed Stephen out of spite. These men secretly persuaded other men to come forward and say, "We have heard Stephen speak blasphemy against Moses and God." This stirred up the people in the religious community and they brought Stephen before the Sanhedrin.

Stephen's countenance changed when he stood before these elders. His face shined like the face of an angel as he listened to false witnesses come forward to testify against him.

When they finished speaking their lies, the high priest questioned Stephen and asked, "Are these charges true?"

Stephen didn't answer him directly. He spoke as a scholar, recounting Jewish history from Abraham to Solomon, then he boldly said, "You stiff-necked people. Nothing has changed over time. You are just like your fathers. You live like the godless nations around you. You firmly stand against the Holy Spirit. Was there ever a prophet your fathers did not persecute? They even killed the prophets who predicted the coming of the Righteous One. And now you have betrayed and killed him."

The Sanhedrin exploded with anger when Stephen condemned them with his words. They were furious and gnashed their teeth at him.

Stephen's life was at risk, yet he stood with courage as if he were by himself speaking to the Holy Spirit. He looked to Heaven and said to the mad men, "Look with me. I see Heaven open and the Son of Man is standing at the right hand of God."

The elders lost control at this point. They covered their ears to mask Stephen's words and yelled at the top of their voices, "Stone him!"

The mob rushed Stephen and dragged him outside the city. They laid their cloaks at the feet of a young Pharisee named Saul (Paul) and began to throw stones. Stephen prayed through the pain as rocks pummeled his body.

When a large stone struck his head, this extraordinary man fell to his knees and cried out, "Lord Jesus, receive my spirit. Please do not hold this sin against these men." When these words passed his lips, Stephen fell asleep for good.

Saul was emboldened by the finality attached to Stephen's murder. He walked away from Stephen's body and began to destroy the church at Jerusalem. He led a great persecution against the congregation of believers that began the day the Sanhedrin killed Stephen. He went from house to house and dragged off men and women to put them in prison. Everyone, except us, quickly scattered throughout Judea and Samaria to escape Saul's persecution.

Stephen was a man full of faith and the Holy Spirit. He was highly regarded by the apostles and the people. The word of God spread while Stephen and others ministered to the widows and the poor. The number of disciples in Jerusalem increased quickly, and many priests became obedient to the faith through the apostles teaching.

Despite Stephen's faith in God and the congregation of believers' faith in him, he was brutally murdered because he dared to argue with evil men cloaked in religion. His death triggered a great persecution that set back the church in Jerusalem.

The apostles' emotions shifted that day from joy, to anger, to grief as they buried Stephen and witnessed the church in Jerusalem implode at Saul's hand.

They suffered the same emotional swing the day they watched Jesus enter Jerusalem. The crowd had praised Jesus as they shouted, "Hosanna, King of Israel." But then they witnessed these same people turn on him and shout, "Barabbas," and sentence Jesus to a grave.

I believe every life has a purpose, and every life is precious in God's sight. Jesus taught about his impending death right before he joined his disciples for the last supper. Jesus spoke with authority, saying, "The time has come for the Son of Man to be glorified in death. Do not be sad when I leave you. I am like the kernel of wheat that falls to the ground. Unless the kernel dies, it remains a single seed. If it dies, it raises from the ground in new life as many seeds."

I don't know why good lives are taken in tragic accidents or senseless acts of violence. And I don't know why God allows His children to suffer at the hand of evil. I do know this: God's children never leave our Father's grasp.

Stephen's murder wasn't wasted life. The believers left their homes in Jerusalem to begin new lives in new lands with the gospel of Jesus Christ in their hearts and minds.

Same God, New Location

Acts 8:4-25

Saul hoped to squelch the gospel message through intimidation when he destroyed the church in Jerusalem. God had a different plan. The apostles simply moved the church underground, and the congregation of believers scattered to new territory, advancing the name of Jesus by preaching the word of God wherever they went.

Philip and Stephen were good friends in Jerusalem. They spent a good part of their days together sharing in the ministry to the widows and the poor.

Philip walked from Jerusalem to Samaria to escape Saul's wrath. When he reached a city in Samaria, God gave him the mantle of evangelist. He proclaimed the good news of Jesus Christ and performed many miraculous signs. The city filled with joy, and the people listened closely to Philip's words as they witnessed him cast out demons and heal the crippled who lived in their communities.

A man named Simon practiced sorcery in the city and throughout Samaria. All the people, both high and low, paid attention to Simon because he had amazed them with his magic for a long time. The Samaritans believed he had divine power and called him "The Great Power." Simon was a crafty wizard who lived his adult life practicing in the spirit world. When he met Philip, he followed him everywhere, astonished by the signs and miracles he saw. Simon made a profession of faith and was baptized along with the other men and women when Philip preached to them the gospel of Jesus Christ.

When we heard that Samaria had accepted the word of God, Peter and I left Jerusalem and went to them. Philip baptized the new believers in the name of the Lord Jesus, but they did not receive the baptism of the Holy Spirit. When we arrived, we prayed for them because the Holy Spirit had not come to anyone. We laid hands on each believer and they received the Holy Spirit.

Simon was mesmerized by the power of God in us. He was amazed that God's Spirit could be gifted to a person through our hands. He came to us and offered to buy our gift with money. Then he said, "Give me this ability so everyone I lay hands on will receive the Holy Spirit."

Peter answered Simon and said, "May your money perish with you because you thought you could buy a gift of God! You will have no part in this ministry because your heart is not right before God. I can see you are full of bitterness and captive to sin. Repent of this wickedness and pray to the Lord. Perhaps He will forgive you."

Philip's friend, Stephen, was brutally murdered because he spoke God's word to the wrong people. Philip lost his home, his friends, his church, and his ministry when Saul turned his attention from Stephen to persecute the congregation of believers.

Like Stephen, Philip was a man full of faith and the Holy Spirit. He was sad when he saw the chaos around him, but he accepted this life change with faith that God would deliver him to a new life. He packed his belongings and walked to Samaria with the gifts God provided him.

When he arrived in Samaria, he accepted a new role and started over at a new location with the God he loved. Philip didn't plan for change in Jerusalem, but he embraced the new life he received, and Samaria accepted the word of God.

When God moves us, the circumstances are rarely fun, and sometimes lonely. Consider it pure joy when we face these trials. Keep your eyes and heart open. God will bring about the adventure of new life through the Holy Spirit when we focus on Him.

Philip and the
Ethiopian Eunuch

Acts 8:26-40, 5:32

Philip enjoyed a lazy morning. He sat by the city well and watched people draw water for their households.

Before long, an angel of the Lord came to him and said, "Philip, go south on the desert road that goes down from Jerusalem to Gaza."

Philip didn't hesitate. He gathered his belongings, left the city, and started out on a new journey. On his way, Philip saw a man in the distance who was sitting in his chariot reading. Philip continued to walk the desert road until Spirit told him, "Go to that chariot and stay near it."

Philip ran to the chariot and heard the man reading Isaiah the prophet. Philip greeted the man and learned he was an Ethiopian eunuch. The man was an important government official who oversaw the Ethiopian queen's treasury. The eunuch had gone to Jerusalem to worship and was now on his way home.

The men carried on a casual conversation for a few minutes, then Philip pointed to the scroll in the eunuch's hand and asked, "Do you understand what you are reading?"

The eunuch answered Philip and said, "Not really. I need someone to explain this passage of scripture to me. Is the prophet speaking about himself or someone else?"

Philip smiled and said, "Perhaps I can be of assistance." The Ethiopian man returned Philip's smile and invited Philip to travel with him in the chariot.

Philip situated himself in the chariot next to the Ethiopian eunuch. When they were ready, the driver guided the horses back onto the dusty road and they headed toward Gaza.

Philip guided the man from Ethiopia through the scripture he was reading, then they shared in a lengthy conversation about Jesus. When Philip finished discussing the good news, the man repented of his sins and believed in the name of Jesus Christ.

As they traveled along the road, the Ethiopian eunuch pointed up ahead toward a pool of water and said, "Look Philip. There is water. Will you please baptize me?"

Philip answered the new believer and said, "Of course, I will be honored to baptize you in the name of the Lord Jesus."

When the chariot came beside the water, the Ethiopian gave orders to stop the horses. Both men entered the water and Philip baptized this influential man from Ethiopia. They rejoiced as they came up out of the water together.

One moment Philip walked beside his new friend experiencing pure joy. The next moment the Spirit of the Lord took Philip away to a new place. The eunuch never saw Philip again, but he took the gospel message home as he continued to rejoice.

Philip appeared again in Azotus and traveled north, preaching the gospel in all the towns until he reached Caesarea, in Judea.

Philip was not an apostle. He was simply a man full of faith and the Holy Spirit who was prepared to act when God called his name.

Philip was a long way from Jerusalem when Spirit spoke to him, and an influential government official carried the gospel message to a foreign land.

God does not ask us to act alone when He calls our name. He gives the gifts we need to those who obey Him.

Are we prepared to act when God calls our name? If not, what holds us back?

Road to Damascus

Acts 9:1-19

Saul breathed murderous threats against the Lord's disciples as he led the great persecution against us in Jerusalem and then, Damascus. As he prepared to leave Jerusalem, he asked Caiaphas to write letters to the synagogues in Damascus giving him permission to transport the disciples in their city to the Jerusalem prison. He wanted the Damascus believers in Jerusalem, so he could obtain a death sentence at trial before the full Sanhedrin.

Saul was possessed with a deep hatred for Jesus and the congregation of believers. His venom spilled onto his men as they traveled together on the road to Damascus.

As they neared the city, a powerful light flashed from Heaven and overwhelmed Saul. The light's energy knocked him off his feet.

As Saul laid on the dusty soil, he absolutely understood for the first time the difference between man and his Creator, and the futility of fighting on the wrong side of the living God.

Saul rose from the road on his elbows and knees. His world was black when he cleared his head. Suddenly, he heard a voice say to him, "Saul. Saul, why do you persecute me?"

Saul reached out his hand into the dark and asked, "Who are you, Lord?"

The voice replied, "I am Jesus, whom you are persecuting. Now get up and go into the city, and you will be told what to do."

Saul had a friend in Damascus named Judas who had a house on Straight Street. Saul instructed his men to leave him with Judas and return to Jerusalem.

Saul remained blind in Judas' home for three days. Saul prayed in the black void, and the Lord spoke to him through visions. He did not eat or drink anything while he waited on the Lord.

We had a disciple in Damascus named Ananias. The Lord came to him in a vision and said, "Ananias!" The disciple was not afraid when Jesus called to him. He knew the Lord's voice.

He answered Jesus and said, "Yes, Lord."

Jesus told him, "Ananias, go to Judas' home on Straight Street and ask for a man from Tarsus, named Saul. I appeared to him on the road from Jerusalem to Damascus three days ago. He is blind and fervently prays for forgiveness. Saul has seen you in a vision. I've told him this man's name is Ananias, and he will come to you and restore your sight by placing his hand on you."

"Lord," Ananias answered, "Saul has done great harm to the disciples in Jerusalem, and now he is in Damascus. He has authority from the chief priests to arrest everyone in Damascus who calls on your name."

Jesus answered Ananias and said, "Go! Saul is my chosen mouthpiece to carry the gospel to the Gentiles and Israel. He is not your problem. I will show him how much he must suffer for my name."

"Your will be done, Lord," Ananias said as the vision ended.

He gathered his cloak and walked to Judas's house. He knocked on the door and asked for Saul. Judas brought Saul into the room where Ananias stood and left. Ananias placed his hand on Saul and said, "Jesus, who appeared to you on the road to Damascus, has sent me here so you may see again and be filled with the Holy Spirit."

When Ananias spoke these words, something like scales dropped from Saul's eyes and he could see.

They left Judas's house together, and Saul was baptized in the name of Jesus.

Saul breathed murderous threats against the Lord's disciples as he wreaked havoc on the lives of believers. Jesus put a stop to Saul's mayhem when the living God confronted him outside Damascus. A vengeful God would have killed Saul on the road to Damascus for the harm he caused His children. But our God saved Saul's life. He saw Saul's gifts and used his zeal, intelligence, and strength to carry the gospel throughout the known world.

If God will forgive Saul's sin, He will forgive our sin. If God will call Saul to perform His mighty works with his history, God can certainly call anyone to service with their past.

Backwash

Acts 9:19-31

Saul was a Pharisee. He was a brilliant man with keen insight into religious law. He listened closely to Jesus when he was alive, and later, he stood in the shadows and listened to Peter and me teach in the temple courts. He knew the gospel story and how it intertwined with God's word. Saul was full of religious knowledge, but he did not know God personally until he confronted Jesus on the road to Damascus.

Believers congregated around Saul for several days in Damascus. They shared a common life. They gave him their resources, studied the scriptures with him, and relived their testimonies. Those men loved Saul because of their love for Jesus Christ.

Saul did not waste time correcting his wrong. He was now filled with the Holy Spirit. Saul immediately went to the synagogues and preached that Jesus is the Son of God.

Saul was bold, but he had no credibility with the people. They said, "Isn't he the one raising havoc in Jerusalem against those who call on Jesus' name? And didn't he come here to take the believers as prisoners to the chief priests?"

Saul silenced the doubters by sharing his conversion story. As he grew more and more powerful, he baffled the religious elite by using God's word to prove Jesus is the Christ.

After many days, the priests and teachers heard enough from Saul. How do you argue with one of your own who is a former Christ hater? They couldn't, so the religious leaders conspired to murder Saul. They watched the city gates day and night to prevent Saul from leaving Damascus.

Saul still had friends in the religious community who told him his life was in danger. They warned him, saying, "Saul, watch your back. You face imminent death in Damascus at the hands of the religious elite."

Saul smiled when he heard this news. He thought to himself, *How quickly life can turn against itself. I was the hunter and now I am the prey. Father, please squash this evil and provide a path to freedom that I may serve you boldly before all men.*

Our friends were familiar with an opening in the city wall. When they heard Saul's life was at risk, they obtained a large basket and took Saul to the city wall that night. They lowered him to the other side in the basket through the hole in the wall.

Then Saul walked back to Jerusalem. When he arrived in the city, he tried to join our disciples, but everyone was afraid of him. No one believed his story. The damage he caused these people was great. They could forgive, but they couldn't forget who this man was. They wouldn't let him near them.

Barnabas was in Damascus for business. He spoke to Ananias and saw Saul preach in the synagogue. He brought Saul to us and said, "Brothers, you should consider spending time with this man. He is no longer the Pharisee we knew. He saw the Lord and Jesus spoke to him on the road to Damascus. He has preached fearlessly in the name of Jesus in the Damascus synagogues."

Barnabas was a man full of faith and filled with the Holy Spirit. We took him at his word and invited Saul into our company.

Saul moved freely about Jerusalem, speaking boldly in the name of Jesus. He spent most of his time talking and debating with the Greek speaking Jews. Like the religious elite in Damascus, they finally heard enough from Saul and tried to kill him.

Saul was no longer our adversary. He was a gift to the congregation of believers. When we learned there was an attempt on his life, we took him to Caesarea and put him on a boat to Tarsus, Saul's birthplace. When Saul left Jerusalem, believers throughout Judea, Galilee, and Samaria enjoyed a time of peace. We were strengthened and encouraged by the Holy Spirit as we grew in numbers and lived with an awe-filled respect for the Lord.

Like many of us, Saul couldn't escape his past as he moved forward in a new life. He was like a boat speeding into smooth harbor water late in the night. The harbor was still. The water was like glass. The other boats sat quietly in their berth. The new boat sped into the harbor on undisturbed water. A large wake followed the boat as it moved to its berth. The new boat easily stopped and docked at its new landing place before the wake hit. Every boat that sat at rest was tossed in its berth by the backwash from the wake the new boat created.

Our Father forgives and forgets our darkest mistakes as we embrace new behavior and attitude, and begin life anew with a transformed heart and mind. God may forgive us, and we may change, but we still live with the results of our past.

People face the backwash of life when they commit shameful, deplorable acts that are utterly wrong. The backwash touches everyone in their circle of love and influence.

People are often not as loving, forgiving, or forgetful of the transgression. How we walk with these people on the journey of forgiveness through the backwash of our mistakes builds the foundation for the new life we hope to live.

Saul patiently waited for the Lord in blindness without complaint. He humbly submitted to strangers' care and hospitality, and immediately corrected his mistake by entering the synagogue and boldly preaching in the name of Jesus Christ. He walked away when the Damascus Jews planned his death. And he accepted the Jerusalem disciples' rejection without argument. All the while God provided a path to freedom that Saul might serve boldly before all men.

Show Up

Acts 9:32-43

Peter traveled throughout the whole country in those days. He preached to the people and ministered to the congregation of believers. On one excursion, God sent Peter to Lydda to heal a man named Aeneas. Aeneas was a believer. He had been paralytic and bedridden for eight years. He prayed for a miracle every night.

When Peter reached Lydda, he asked a stranger, "Please tell me where Aeneas stays." Peter found him at his home and said, "Aeneas, Jesus Christ heals you. Get up and take care of your mat."

Aeneas was full of faith and the Holy Spirit. He praised God for answering his prayers as he rose to his feet. He hugged Peter, and then danced before the Lord.

Peter laughed with joy and his heart was thankful he saw this mighty work of God take place before his eyes.

All the people who lived in Lydda and Sharon saw Aeneas walk the streets. They rejoiced with him as he told his story of answered prayers. The people in both towns turned from their unbelief when they saw Aeneas and followed the name of Jesus Christ.

Tabitha lived in Joppa. Lydda was a short distance from Joppa. Tabitha was a disciple of great reputation among the believers. She helped the poor and always assisted others with a servant's heart. Tabitha became sick and died while Peter was in Lydda.

When the disciples in Joppa learned Peter was nearby, they sent two men to Peter and urged him, saying, "Please come at once. Tabitha became sick and died."

Peter gathered his belongings and walked with the men to Joppa. On the way, he remembered how Jesus raised Lazarus from the dead. Peter also remembered how Jesus' spirit groaned. God's involvement in that mighty miracle was evident to everyone.

Peter was concerned. He talked to God as he recalled Lazarus coming forth from the tomb. He thought, *Lord, these people are full of faith. They anticipate a miracle today. The disciples expect Tabitha to rise from the dead. I am just a man. Jesus is Your Son. He called Lazarus back to life through your power in him. Father, do I have the power to raise the dead?*

When Peter finished his thought, the Holy Spirit prompted him with Jesus' words to Peter, me, and the other disciples. Peter said, "I leave you now, but when I am gone, I will send you the Holy Spirit. The works you have seen me do, greater works you will do through the Holy Spirit who will be in you and with you. Do you believe?"

Peter smiled and quickened his pace as he thought, *I believe I can do all things you ask of me, Lord, in your name.*

Spirit's voice responded to Peter then, saying, "Go to Tabitha, Peter. God will wake her from her sleep in your presence."

Tabitha's house was full of grief. As soon as Peter arrived, the people who mourned her took him to Tabitha in the upper room. He consoled the weeping widows who stood around him before he asked everyone in the room to leave. When Peter was alone with Tabitha, he fell to his knees beside her bed and prayed for her life in the name of Jesus Christ.

Peter was filled with God's power in the Holy Spirit. He turned to Tabitha and said, "Get up."

Tabitha opened her eyes, and seeing Peter, she smiled and sat up in the bed. Peter took her hands and helped her to her feet.

When Tabitha was stable, Peter called to the house and everyone came to the upper room. The room filled with Spirit as everyone joined together to praise God for this mighty miracle. Their beloved friend had returned to them.

This good news spread throughout Joppa and more people believed in the Lord.

God told Peter to stay in the city with a tanner named Simon.

Peter was anxious as he walked to Joppa. The disciples in Tabitha's house expected a miracle that exceeded the scope of his imagination. Yes, he was just a man; but he was a person full of faith and the Holy Spirit who showed up when Spirit's voice spoke to him. He didn't believe in his own gifts and talents to complete God's work, but he knew he could do all things God asked of him, in Jesus' name.

Peter's faith in Jesus did not grow from quiet reflection in the morning, moments of prayer during the day, and scripture reading at night. Peter gained his confidence in God's love and power pouring through him by living with Jesus every day for three years and seeing the Holy Spirit act through him and the other apostles in Jerusalem.

Faith-based living begins when God calls us to complete a task and we show up. Just like Peter, we can do all things God asks of us, in Jesus' name. We too can laugh with joy as our heart fills with gratitude when we watch the works of God take place before our eyes.

Show up and see!

No Man Is Unclean
or Impure

Acts 10:1-23, 28

Cornelius was a centurion. He was the commander of one hundred men in the Roman army stationed at Caesarea. He and his family had a zeal for the Lord, but they were not members of the Jewish faith.

Cornelius prayed to our Father regularly and was known in Caesarea for his generosity to the poor. One day about three o'clock in the afternoon, Cornelius sat in his back yard enjoying his garden when an angel of God came to him in a vision. The angel said, "Cornelius!"

Cornelius was a warrior among men, but he was frightened by the angel of God. He had never seen a celestial being. He stared at the angel until he regained his wits, then he asked, "What can I do for you, Lord?"

The angel answered Cornelius and said, "Your prayers and your gifts to the poor have risen to Heaven as a memorial offering before God. Because you are faithful, God calls you to complete a task for Him. There is a man in Joppa named Simon Peter. He stays with Simon the tanner at a house by the sea. Send men to Joppa to bring Peter to your home. He will speak God's words to you and your family."

When the angel left, Cornelius remained in the back yard. He was very excited as he reconciled his faith with his reality—Cornelius worshiped a living God. He rejoiced for a time, then went into the house and called two of his servants and a devout soldier to his side. He shared everything that happened with them, then sent the men to Joppa to bring back Peter.

Peter was hungry and asked a servant for his midday meal about noon the following day. It was Peter's routine to climb the steps to Simon's roof and kneel to pray while his meal was prepared.

Cornelius' men approached Joppa as Peter kneeled in solitude on the roof. He fell into a trance while he prayed. Peter saw Heaven open and a sheet came down to earth by its four corners. The sheet was full of four-footed animals, reptiles of the earth, and birds of the sky. A voice said to him, "Peter, get up. Kill and eat."

Peter said in his defiant manner, "No way, Lord. I have never eaten anything impure or unclean."

The voice spoke a second time, saying, "Do not call anything impure that God has made clean."

This happened three times, then the sheet was taken back to heaven.

When the trance broke, Peter stood on the roof and stared out to sea. He thought to himself, *Why did I receive this vision?*

At the same time Peter was contemplating the vision, the men from Caesarea found Simon's house. They came to the outside gate and called out, asking, "Does Simon who is known as Peter stay here?"

The Spirit said to Peter, "Simon, three men are downstairs looking for you. Go greet them. Do not hesitate to leave with them when they ask. I have sent them to you."

Peter hurried down the stairs, went out the front door and greeted the travelers at the front gate. He said, "I am Peter. Why have you come?"

The men replied, "Our home is in Caesarea. Cornelius the centurion sent us to you with a message. He is a righteous man of God who is respected by the Jewish people in our community. An angel of God spoke to him about you and said, 'Send men to Joppa to bring Peter to your home. He will speak God's words to you and your family.'"

Peter paused to consider the Gentiles request and thought, *Jewish law forbids its people to associate with or visit a Gentile. Yet the Spirit has commanded me to leave with these men.* God's vision became clear to Peter when he finished this thought. No man is unclean or impure in God's eyes.

Simon Peter's heart quickened as he realized in thought God's next step for the congregation of believers and the apostles: *We are going into the whole world to preach the good news of Jesus Christ to all people.*

Simon Peter relaxed. He greeted the travelers with a friendly smile, opened the front gate for the Gentiles and extended a warm welcome to his home. He said, "Thank you for walking this distance to deliver this message. I look forward to speaking with Cornelius and his family. I'm sure you are weary from your travels. Stay the night with me at my home as my guests and we will leave for Caesarea in the morning."

Cornelius was a Gentile, a Roman Centurion who lived in Caesarea. And God loved Cornelius.

How could God love Cornelius? The Roman centurion wasn't a Jew, and he wasn't a member of the congregation of believers scattered to Caesarea from Jerusalem. He was simply a Gentile who loved our Father.

Why love Cornelius? The answer is straightforward. God loves each person as a person. His affection is not bound by tradition, religion, status, privilege, race, sex, inheritance, geography, or sin.

God helped Peter understand that no one is unclean or impure in our Father's eyes. God seeks a spiritual relationship with anyone who will worship Him in spirit and truth. Peter relaxed with this new truth. He gladly welcomed his Gentile guests into his home and then he began to imagine a world-wide ministry that shared the good news of Jesus Christ with all people.

Prejudice

Acts 11:1-18

Peter walked for two days on the road from Joppa to Caesarea to reach Cornelius' home. Cornelius invited his relatives and close friends to his residence in anticipation of Peter's arrival. When the apostle came through Cornelius' front door, the centurion fell at Peter's feet in reverence.

Peter was embarrassed by this outward display of respect and made the man get up. He said, "Cornelius, please stand up. I am only a man myself."

The Gentile stood up, gave Peter a hug, welcomed him to his home, and then guided him into a large room filled with people.

Cornelius introduced the apostle to the gathering. Then Peter said, "May I ask why you sent for me?"

The centurion shared his vision in detail with the people in the room. Then he said to Peter, "When the angel of God spoke to me, I sent for you immediately, and it is good that you have come. Now we are all here in the presence of God to listen to everything the Lord has commanded you to tell us."

Cornelius sat down beside his wife and children as Peter began to speak. He said: "I know it's true now. God does not show favoritism toward one person over another. He accepts men of all nations who fear him and do what is right. You know the message God sent to the people of Israel, telling the good news of peace through Jesus Christ, who is Lord of all. You know what happened throughout Judea, beginning with Galilee after the baptism that John preached and how God anointed Jesus with the power of the Holy Spirit. Jesus performed mighty works and healed all who were under Satan's power because God was with him. The apostles witnessed everything Jesus did in the country of the Jews and in Jerusalem. They killed him by nailing him to a cross, but God raised him from the dead on the third day and we saw him. We ate with

Jesus and drank with Jesus after he rose from the dead. He has commanded us to preach to the people and testify that he is the One God appointed to judge the living and the dead. Everyone who believes in Jesus receives forgiveness of sins through his name."

Cornelius' family and friends were listening intently to Peter testify when the Holy Spirit came on everyone who heard Peter speak. The people praised God and spoke in tongues, the same as the Jewish believers did on the day of Pentecost.

Six Jewish believers accompanied Peter from Joppa. They did not rejoice with the other people in the room. They were astonished when the Holy Spirit came upon the Gentiles. They still believed the Jews were God's chosen people.

Peter's heart was troubled by these men's reaction. He pulled them to the side and said, "How can you be so arrogant? Do you oppose God? These precious people have received the Holy Spirit just as we have."

Peter looked to the crowded room and saw people filled with joy worship God with words of praise and thanksgiving. He turned to the six men with anger in his eyes and said, "Can anyone keep these people from being baptized with water?"

No one dared to argue with Peter, so he ordered these people be baptized in the name of Jesus Christ.

Jewish believers throughout Judea heard the Gentiles received the word of God. They did not rejoice. Just like the six men from Joppa, the Jewish believers were born to understand they were God's chosen people. They were taught from an early age Gentiles were lesser people. It was troubling for them to hear the Gentiles had encroached upon their birthright.

When Peter returned to Jerusalem with the six men from Joppa, he was criticized. The Jewish believers reprimanded him, saying, "You went into the house of uncircumcised men and you ate with them."

Peter sat down with us and explained everything precisely as it happened. He described Cornelius' encounter with the angel of God, his vision on Simon the tanner's roof top, and the Holy Spirit coming to the Gentiles in Cornelius' home.

He said, "As I began to speak, the Holy Spirit came on them as He came on us in the beginning. Then I remembered what the Lord had said, 'John baptized with water, but you will be baptized with the Holy Spirit.' So, if God gave them the same gift He gave us, who am I to oppose God?"

When Peter finished telling his story, we had no more objections. We all praised God and said, "So then, God has granted the Gentiles repentance unto life."

Jesus asked Peter to lead the congregation of believers. He was respected by all for his faith and the power of the Holy Spirit he exhibited through his words and the miraculous works he completed with God. Even Peter was filled with prejudice against the Gentiles until God turned his mind and heart. Peter and Cornelius looked past their lifetime beliefs and obeyed Spirit's voice. God used these men to breakdown centuries of prejudice to reveal Himself to the Gentile world.

How deep do our prejudices run? No one is a chosen person, and no one is a lesser person. Only God judges; not us. We are at our best when we live a humble life before the Lord, loving everyone as God loves us. We rejoice when glad tidings come to the other person and we extend a helping hand to those in need.

Share goodness and be grateful we do not walk in another person's shoes.

Antioch

Acts 11:19-30

Believers caught in Saul's great persecution scattered from Jerusalem and traveled as far away as Phoenicia, Cyprus, and Antioch. They congregated at synagogues along the way and delivered Jesus' message to the Jewish population. Some of the Jewish believers from Cyprus and Cyrene eventually moved on to Antioch and began to share their message with the Greeks in the community. God placed His hand on the city of Antioch, and the city watched a great number of the Greek citizens turn to the Lord.

We heard the good news from Antioch and sent Barnabas to teach the new believers and care for the new church. Barnabas was a good man, full of the Holy Spirit and faith. When he arrived in the city, he was surrounded by young believers, filled with God's grace, who hungered for God's word.

Barnabas was glad in his heart to live like Jesus with the Gentiles.

Some new believers, who walked alone before Barnabas arrived, waivered in their new faith. Barnabas encouraged everyone to remain true to the Lord with all their hearts.

When he preached, a greater number of Gentiles came to the Lord. The magnitude of ministry became too great for one man, so Barnabas walked to Tarsus to find Saul. They both stayed in Antioch for one year teaching the disciples in the growing church.

Prophets came from Jerusalem to Antioch while Barnabas and Saul pastored the church. Agabus was one of the prophets. He stood up before the congregation when he was filled with the Holy Spirit. He predicted a severe famine would spread over the entire Roman world.

The church was deeply concerned for the Jewish believers in Judea. The church came together as one body and agreed they would each provide help for the Christians living in Judea. The church collected an offering and sent their gift to us through Barnabas and Saul.

It's ironic to watch God's hand move at Antioch, the first place to use the name Christian. The Jewish men and women at Cyprus and Cyrene held a deep prejudice against the Greeks when they departed Jerusalem. These believers and their families left the people they knew and the life they understood in Jerusalem, to follow God's Spirit to Antioch. They made a home for themselves with the Greeks and the church grew exponentially.

Who could guess a church filled with Gentile believers would send a meaningful financial gift to support the Jewish believers in Jerusalem?

Saul instigated the great persecution in Jerusalem that drove these Jewish believers to seek a new life among new people in a new culture. Who could predict Saul would be their co-pastor at the Church of Antioch?

Who are we to judge God when our lives turn over? The Israelites questioned God when He brought them from Egypt to take them to the Promised Land. When the people complained, God realized their character lacked the quality needed to take the Promised Land. He cared for the Israelites where they complained, but they remained in the wilderness instead of the Promised Land until that generation died.

The congregation of believers did not grieve when they left their comfort zone during the great persecution. They remained steadfast while following the Holy Spirit and resting in our Father's grasp. The believers did not panic when their lives turned over in a foreign land with a different culture over a short period of time.

God was glorified in the new life He delivered to the congregation of believers. They loved God and their neighbors as themselves. They placed their future in God's hands. They obeyed Spirit's voice. And they witnessed a mighty work of God performed through them.

Bad Things Will Happen to Good People

Acts 12:1-25

King Herod was a worldly man consumed with carnal desires. He derived pleasure persecuting the church in Jerusalem during the Feast of Unleavened Bread. He beheaded my brother, James, with a sword blade, and he had several other church members thrown in prison.

When Herod saw this pleased the Jews, he upped the game he played with us and had Peter arrested. Herod set Peter to the side and made plans to present him for public trial after the Passover.

Herod didn't forget Peter and I escaped from his prison the last time we were placed in a Jerusalem jail cell. He beefed up security to prevent Peter's escape now. After his arrest, Peter was handed over to four squads of four soldiers each.

The night before his trial, Peter was asleep between two soldiers, bound with two chains, while sentries stood guard in front of his cell door and the other prison doors that led to the city gate. Sometime during the night, a light shone in the cell and an angel appeared.

The angel struck Peter on the side and woke him up. He said, "Quick, get up, put your clothes on, and follow me."

The chains dropped from Peter's wrists and the apostle dressed. Peter followed the angel, but he thought he was seeing a vision. The angel guided Peter through the prison, out the gate into the city, and down the full length of one street before he suddenly disappeared.

When the angel left, Peter realized he wasn't seeing a vision. He thought to himself, *There is no doubt the Lord sent His angel to rescue me from Herod and the Jewish people's torture.*

Peace in the Jerusalem church came to an end. Believers feared Herod's unpredictable nature. They saw Herod kill James on a whim. Peter was next. And more believers waited their death sentence in the public prison. People gathered at Mary's home and earnestly prayed to God for Peter's wellbeing. (Mary was Mark's mother.)

Peter walked to Mary's house while the city slept and knocked on the locked door. Everyone was astonished when they saw Peter. Earlier in our ministry, Peter and I escaped from jail. The believers rejoiced that God had sent an angel to secure his release a second time.

Peter described to them how the Lord brought him out of prison, then he said, "Tell James (Jesus' brother), and the others about this."

When he finished sharing how he escaped Herod's grasp, he hugged his faithful friends and smiled, then he walked by himself into the night.

In the morning, the prison was in chaos. The soldiers searched everywhere to find Peter. Herod came to the prison and had the soldiers search again with the same result. He cross-examined each soldier to discern the truth. Then he ordered that they all be executed.

Herod left from Judea for Caesarea in frustration to finish business he had with the people of Tyre and Sidon. On the appointed day, he dressed in his royal robe, sat on his throne, and delivered a speech to the public.

When Herod concluded his address, the people shouted, "This is the voice of God, not man."

Herod made no effort to refute the claim to his deity. At that moment, an angel of the Lord struck him down with violent pain because he did not give praise to God. Herod was eaten by worms from the inside. Days later, he died.

While all this was taking place, Barnabas and Saul returned to Jerusalem to deliver the gift from the church at Antioch. We all rejoiced when we heard the good news coming from the ministry to the Gentiles and how the word of God continued to spread despite the persecution we faced. When Barnabas and Saul finished their mission, they returned to Antioch with Mark.

A person's decision to claim the name of Jesus Christ and worship our Father in spirit and truth was not a casual choice. John the Baptist was beheaded. Jesus was crucified. Stephen was stoned to death. James was beheaded. The church at Jerusalem was scattered by persecution. Peter and I were imprisoned. And the remnant in Jerusalem continued to face persecution at Herod's hand.

Despite evil's best effort, God's Spirit wasn't stopped. God's word spread to the world, and the congregation of believers grew in number.

All this death and suffering reminds me of the day Gamaliel counseled the Sanhedrin on our behalf. He stated, "It's in the Sanhedrin's best interest to leave these men alone. If their purpose comes from human origin, it will fail. It always does. But if their purpose is God's, we will not be able to stop these men. If we try, we will find ourselves fighting God."

Jesus did not establish his earthly kingdom when he came to the disciples, and believers on earth do not live in paradise with Jesus Christ now. We live in an unpredictable world where dark spirits continue to steal and destroy people's innocence. The wicked do not discriminate.

Why would evil ignore the blameless who are full of faith and the Holy Spirit? Satan and his army inflict hardship and pain wherever they can.

Peter walked with Jesus for three years and he led the first church in Jerusalem. Although he healed the sick and raised a woman from the dead, he sat in a secure prison and awaited an uncertain future because Herod saw it pleased the Jews. Sixteen soldiers watched over Peter when God sent an angel of the Lord to rescue him from Herod's clutches.

When adversity comes our way, why be a slave to fear? We are God's children, and our Father holds us in His grasp.

If our purpose comes from God, we are not alone to face disappointment, confusion, or sorrow by ourselves. If we own the purpose, then we cause the adversity with our actions.

We all make mistakes, some small, others colossal. When we do, we can quietly turn to the Lord in meekness to face our trials with the love, strength, integrity, and understanding the Holy Spirit can provide us.

Although we make mistakes when we set God aside to live alone, our love and life will stand out for all to plainly see if we humbly work hard to make amends.

Our Father's Spirit Illuminates

I John 1-10, 2:1-8, 15-17

Half a century has passed since I walked with Jesus and the other apostles. Sharing life with the congregation of believers in Jerusalem is a fond memory. I live in Ephesus now and minister to the churches in the province of Asia (modern Turkey). I tell my story to you from Ephesus as an old man so my joy may be complete.

My life is different, and the people I serve has changed with it, but the message I share with you from Jesus Christ remains the same. God's Spirit is Life and in Him there is no evil at all. He loves those born of His Spirit as a father loves his children. The Father knows how we feel and think, and He understands better than anyone our strengths and our struggles.

God breathed life into us at conception, and He's fully aware He's placed us in a culture that rejects His love and the eternal life He offers. He gifts us His spirit to illuminate our thinking as we love our neighbors, grow in His gifts, and overcome our mistakes and disappointments.

Our Father communicates His truth to us as He separates His children from a worldly lifestyle to protect us from Satan and to bear witness to people in our life that our words, works, and love come through Him.

You must know, I am deeply concerned for the church's integrity and well-being. False teachers now lead you astray with a twisted gospel message that appeals to your carnal nature.

They tell you God judges the spirit, not the flesh. If you are born of Spirit, you do not sin. These wicked men say, "God's children are free to pursue immoral lives in this lifetime as they enjoy God's fellowship from death to life and onto eternal life."

I say to you, "Anyone who believes this teaching deceives themselves and God's truth is not in them."

We fool ourselves if we believe wickedness exists in God. The Holy Spirit is the gate that separates a spiritual life with God from a worldly life without God.

God's spirit is squelched in those who act on the false teacher's message. If we assume we can claim a life with God and still live a worldly lifestyle apart from God's truth, we lie to ourselves and do not live in His authenticity.

My dear children, when we live apart from God, we lay ourselves open to the thief who will destroy what is good in us. At a certain point in time, great pain will occur when our secrets are exposed to our circle of life.

I encourage everyone to come back to what we know is true. Do not love the world or anything in the world. If we love the world, the love of the Father is not in us. For everything in the world—the cravings of sinful people, the lust of their eyes and the boasting of what they have and do—doesn't come from the Father, but from the world. The world and its desires pass away, but the ones who do the will of God live forever.

You tell me, "I know God. He is my Father and I am His child." Heaven rejoices. This is God's desire for all who come to Him through His son, Jesus Christ.

We know we have grasped who God is with clarity and certainty when we return our Father's love and we practice what it means to listen to His voice and honor His commands.

God's love is completed in us for our world to see as we trust His truth and we live within Spirit's illumination. If a person says, "I know God," but the person goes their own way ignoring God's voice, the person lies to themselves and the truth is not in them. This is how we are certain God is in us and with us—we live our life as Jesus lived his life.

I wish we didn't ignore the Holy Spirit and walk away to live without God in our lives, but we do. Sometimes the guilt and shame attached to our choices are so detrimental, we are too ashamed to return to our Father and the ones we have harmed to ask for their healing forgiveness. It seems easier to fall deeper into our secret world to mask our pain than face God as He stands in our path calling our name with open arms.

Each time we take a step away from God, it becomes easier. We hardly recognize Satan has killed our joy and destroyed what is good in us as we live outside God's love and gifts. Before long, God's voice disappears, and we are left alone to stumble through life in blindness, shrouded in harmful emotions we accumulate in the dark world.

We may spiral down in darkness, but we are never lost in this lifetime. Jesus Christ is our advocate. When we call his name, Spirit will find us and love us as we are at that moment. He will bring us home. He fights for those he loves. He is our defender.

When we confess our sins and return to God, no matter the sin, Jesus Christ speaks to the Father in our defense.

God doesn't ask us to make a sacrifice for our sins. He doesn't punish us, and He is deeply saddened when we punish ourselves.

Jesus made amends for our sins before we were born through his sacrifice on the cross. And not just our sins, but everyone's sins. Our mistakes are forgiven and forgotten by God through the name of Jesus Christ.

Hatred Blinds People

I John 2:9-11, John 17:20-24

I watched over Jesus at the Mount of Olives as he prayed. When he finished his prayer for my brothers, he stood among us for a few minutes then he returned to his place and began to pray for all believers to come. He said, "Father, my prayer is for all those who will believe in me through the disciples' ongoing message. May they be one as you and I are one. May they be in complete unity to show the world you sent me, and you love them as you love me."

We achieve unity as one when everyone walks with the Holy Spirit in His illumination and love. God brings us together as spirit-filled individuals with one voice to share our Father's love and gifts in times of worship, service, refreshment, and sorrow. We reflect His love to our family, friends, co-workers, and neighbors when our countenance is filled by the Holy Spirit with characteristics like love, strength, integrity, praise, charity, wisdom, compassion, patience, empathy, mercy, and sacrifice.

I am saddened to hear we have church members who hate each other. How did this happen? Don't you know hatred blinds people?

You are fools to believe Spirit lives in people who stumble about with open hatred in their heart. Hatred causes irrevocable harm as haters succumb to evil ways without any idea where they go. This behavior must stop now. Work hard to discover the underlying factors that cause this behavior and resolve it promptly before evil collapses in on everyone.

Some people hate, but at what cost? These people lose themselves as they turn inward to focus on their frustration, strife, jealousy, resentment, anger, and hatred. Haters cannot see what others witness, as their hearts harden before our eyes.

We've seen hatred's results, and it rarely ends in happiness.

We will live for a time or seasons, but we will not live forever. Life is a gift, and how we live for ourselves matters. Why waste a single day filled with negative energy that festers in such an unbecoming way and causes so much damage?

We bear witness to our circle of life that we worship a loving God as we love each other with His love. We reflect His love when our countenance is filled by the Holy Spirit with kindness, compassion, and forgiveness.

There should be no place for dark feelings in us. The world expects this harsh behavior. When they experience it with us, they assume there is no God.

Little Children Come to Me

I John 2:15-17, Mark 10:13-27, Matt 18:2-6

I remember a special day, long ago, when we stood with Jesus and listened to him teach multitudes in the land of Judea across from the Jordan River. As he spoke, parents brought their children to Jesus to have him bless their child.

Some of the disciples were deeply offended by this act of love. They stepped forward and rebuked the parents for interrupting the Rabbi's talk.

When Jesus saw this, he called out in a loud voice for all to hear and said, "Let the little children come to me. Do not get in a child's way by obstructing them or delaying their progress. The Kingdom of Heaven belongs to such as these. This is God's truth; everyone who enters the Kingdom of God on their last day comes to Heaven the same way a little child receives a gift."

When Jesus finished admonishing the disciples, he dropped to his knees, opened his arms, and embraced the little ones as they swarmed him. He took each child in his arms. He loved them, then blessed them before he returned them to their parents.

Jesus stood with the last child by his side and addressed the crowd again. He said, "You lust after the things of this world. You feel rich, safe, and secure with your accomplishments and your lifestyle. You strive on your own to improve your position and your possessions in this world at the expense of your relationships and wellbeing.

"I tell you God's truth, unless you change and become as a little child, you will never enter the Kingdom of Heaven. The greatest ones in the Kingdom of Heaven are those who humble themselves like this child and follow Spirit in this lifetime."

Jesus shifted his gaze to the child by his side. He smiled and ruffled his hair. Then he spoke to the crowd again, and said, "If you welcome a little child like this in my name as they come to you, you welcome me. Love them as I love you no matter how or when they come to you.

"Remember, you are not perfect, and neither are they. Accept them as they are with our Father's love in you and they will learn to see themselves as I see them—a child of God, perfect in every way.

"They will grow to love God as the Father loves you—in your arms.

"If anyone causes a little one who believes in me to sin, it would be better for that person to have a large millstone tied around their neck and to be drowned in the depth of the sea."

Jesus spoke God's truth and healed many who were crippled, infirmed, and demon-possessed that day. He finished his work as the sun rested in the late afternoon sky.

As we set out on the road to our lodging, a young ruler ran up to us and fell to his knees before Jesus. He said, "Good teacher, what must I do to inherit eternal life?"

Jesus answered the man and said, "Why do you say I am good? No one is good except God, alone. You know the commandments: Do not murder, do not commit adultery, do not steal, do not give false testimony, do not defraud, honor your mother and father."

"Teacher," the man declared as he interrupted Jesus, "I know the commandments. I have kept them all since I was a boy."

Jesus stared into the man's eyes. He loved him because his mind and heart were innocent. Jesus said to the young ruler, "You speak truth, young man. You have obeyed the commandments. However, there is one thing you lack. You love your wealth and position in society more than you love God. If you seek eternal life, then go sell all your possessions, and give the proceeds to the poor. You will have treasure in Heaven. Then come, follow me."

The young ruler's countenance changed to deep sadness as he listened to Jesus explain what he must do to inherit eternal life. He rose to his feet and walked away from Jesus for good because he was a man of great wealth and status.

The young man chose what he could see, his worldly lifestyle, over what was yet to be seen, an abundant life through Jesus Christ.

People walk away from the Holy Spirit to chase the things of the world. Many are older now. They have watched and learned this truth over their years: Satan uses the lust of our flesh, the lust of our eyes, and the boastful pride of life to snuff out the love of God in us. The energy to live the worldly life passes away, and we are left alone to face our lifetime choices.

Come to Jesus when he first calls to you the same way a little child lives with its loving parents and enjoy the abundant life God gifts to us from death to life and beyond through the Holy Spirit.

False Teachers

I John 2:18-29, John 14:6

God has delivered His truth to His creation through the Son of God. Jesus Christ is the way, the truth, and the life.

God's era of new prophecy and a new path to salvation is over. He has no reason to bring a new word to the world through another voice.

He delivered His seal to us when Jesus Christ poured out the Holy Spirit on the congregation of believers at Pentecost. God's children are now born of His Spirit. The Holy Spirit is God's confirmation the Father is with us and in us in this life as we pass with Him from death to life to the Kingdom of Heaven and on to eternal life.

Dear children, we have heard rumors the antichrist is coming. Even now many false teachers have come to you. They corrupt the gospel taught by the Holy Spirit through the apostles for personal gain.

These people started with us, but they never belonged to us. If they were part of us, they would have remained with us. Their message contradicts God's truth which proves they never belonged to us.

We shouldn't be surprised new teachings have appeared. Worldly people have used God's name to promote themselves throughout history. Godless teachers profit as they establish religions that bring a form of order to life. They appeal to people's social awareness and conscious enlightenment while they describe a pathway to afterlife that supports a worldly lifestyle and brings comfort to their godless following.

Do not let these people turn you from God with their teaching. You do not need another teacher. You have been anointed with truth by the Father through the Holy Spirit.

Antichrists will try to make you believe they worship the heavenly Father. You know there is no lie in God's truth. How do know a teacher is lying? The person denies that Jesus is the Christ. When a person denies the Son, they also deny the Father.

Always remember God's truth: anyone who refuses to believe in the Son rejects the Father because they are one.

The Son of God walked with his creation for three-years. He was a living example of how to live life as he shared God's love and truth through his words and his works.

This false teacher warning was delivered to the churches approximately fifty-years after the outpouring of the Holy Spirit in Jerusalem. It's hard to believe the purity of God's truth did not last through a second generation of believers before antichrists began to twist God's truth with their own teaching.

Here we are, two thousand years later. It's estimated there are roughly 4,200 religions in the world. Antichrists permeate our world. Godless people actively use God's name to turn innocent people from His truth with their opinions. Their religions now consume a large portion of our world population.

I encourage you to live in and with Spirit, so when the final day comes, you are unashamed, and you run to Jesus with open arms.

He Calls Us His Children

I John 3:1-10, John 17:6-16, John 2:13-22

Our God is an awesome God. He is worthy of our praise and devotion. He created the heavens and earth and everything in them. Our God reigns over Heaven and earth. There is no one like Him.

He sent His Son into the world as a lasting sacrifice for our sin, and now that His Son has returned to Heaven, Jesus delivers Spirit to those who believe in his name. The Spirit teaches us how to live an abundant life with the gifts we receive from God.

God protects us and keeps us safe through the power of His Son's name—Jesus Christ. He does not take us out of the world. God protects us from evil as He sends us into the world by separating us from the world with His truth. God's word is truth.

We grow in faith and wisdom as we patiently listen to His voice and trust His Spirit in our daily lives.

God is divine and we are human. How great is the heavenly Father's love for us that He freely gives us the Holy Spirit when we believe in His Son's name?

He calls us His children when we are born of His Spirit. And that is what we are, God's children! We know who we are now, but it has not been revealed to us what we will be when our time here ends. We can believe this truth with complete confidence: we shall be like Jesus because we will see him as he is.

Do not be led astray by false teachers now as they try to sway you with teaching that appeals to the lust of the flesh and eyes, and the boastful pride of life. People will try to convince us a person can be a child of God and continue to live a worldly life of sin. This will always be a bold lie that causes harm to whoever is deceived.

We alienate ourselves from God when we choose to deliberately walk in darkness and disobey our Father's known will for our life.

This is a way we know we are children of God. We set aside our worldly lifestyles and strive to live a life that honors our heavenly Father. How else can the child of God walk with Spirit in the illumination of life? God is Spirit and in Him there is no wickedness.

I'll never forget when we entered the temple courts, and we were overwhelmed by the sound and smell of livestock and the noise of moneychangers. The temple had changed from a holy place of worship into a marketplace where oxen, sheep, and doves were sold; and money was exchanged on the temple courts floor. Jesus was outraged. Devotion to God's House consumed the Son of God. We had never seen Jesus irate. He was very angry with the religious guardians responsible for maintaining this holy place and the marketers earning a profit. Jesus raged against the godless people who turned this uncommon place—a holy place where people were supposed to meet their revered God—into a worldly place where evil had rejected God.

Like the temple guardians in Jerusalem, we are responsible for living lives that honor the generous gifts we receive from the Holy Spirit. We meet God through Spirit who lives in us and with us. When we listen to Spirit's voice, and follow His lead, Spirit illuminates the way to navigate a loveless world consumed by wickedness. We can live an abundant life in the world that honors our Father when we faithfully live in and with Spirit.

Our lives break down when we turn away to pursue a life separate from God.

Don't be surprised when our Father fights to get our attention and bring us home. Jesus raged against the hardened people who turned the place where man meets God into a worldly place where darkness rejected Light. Jesus demanded God's house be returned to a holy place of worship. He gathered rope, made a whip of cords, and unleashed his fury on the marketplace. He overturned tables, spilled coins across the temple floor, then drove the livestock and birds from the temple shouting, "Take these things away! How dare you make my Father's house a market."

Jesus fought hard for God's House. Do you think He cares any less about his children?

Love Your Neighbor
as Yourself

I John 3:10-11, Matt 22:37, Matt 18:21-35

Love the Lord, your God, with all your heart and soul and mind, and love your neighbor as yourself. This is a commandment we have heard since we first received the good news of Jesus Christ.

It's understandable that the God component of this love equation is easier to achieve than brotherly love. God does not wrong us, and He does not break our hearts. God's love is perfect. He loves us with abundance. He never betrays us, abandons us, or stands against us. Although our family, neighbors, co-workers, acquaintances, and confidants can cause us serious pain when they do one or all these things to us, God commands us to love them without condition. He tells us to love them as ourselves despite the chaos they bring to our life.

"Love our neighbors as ourselves," can be hard words to accept; yet living this commandment is a way we know we are children of God.

I was disappointed when I learned there is open hatred between some of you. No matter what is confessed with words, anyone who hates will not enjoy eternal life with God. A person filled with faith and Spirit has no room in their heart for bitter hostility toward another person. If we hate, we separate from God and cause damage to ourselves and others. We know we pass from death to abundant life when we love others as we love ourselves.

Often, loving ourselves and others begins with forgiveness, the same as God forgives us. I remember a day in Capernaum when Jesus was teaching the crowd in parables. Peter and I stood next to Jesus as he finished teaching the people about the brother who sins against him. Peter asked Jesus, "Lord, how many times shall I forgive my brother when he sins against me? Up to seven times?"

Jesus shook his head no and then he said, "I tell you, Peter, not seven times, but seventy-seven times."

Then he said, "Peter, be kind and merciful. Forgive without condition even when others hold grudges or strike back. You don't know the underlying factors causing a person's poor behavior.

"Be a beacon of love in their world. Over time, I will show them wisdom, compassion, patience, empathy, mercy, and sacrifice through you. Love them as I love you. They may see my love is everything they need to calm the stormy sea of their soul."

How do we find the emotional strength to love those who harm us or hate us with the love we have for ourselves? It's difficult when we learn from an early age to withhold our love and protect our heart and mind when we are wronged.

How did Jesus prosper in strength and integrity during his challenging life? He loved deeply those who were so unlovable. He came to the people that they might have life and love and have it abundantly. He didn't depend on these people for emotional security. Jesus shared his heart-of-hearts with his Father and his disciples, and he loved the unlovable people from the overflow of his love for God.

Before we walk into an emotionally charged situation, trust Spirit. Be slow to speak while we listen closely, and Spirit will illuminate the way to love and respond. When we follow Spirit, we can love the unlovable from the overflow of our love for God. We are not responsible for how we are loved and liked in return.

Be Careful to Whom You Listen and Follow

I John 3:19-24, 4:1-6

Dear friends, the spirit of the antichrist is raging spiritual warfare in our world. Be careful to whom you listen and follow. Test every spirit. The apostle's testimony has been twisted over the years, and false prophets now declare that Jesus either did not come in the flesh or he did not come from God. These are both lies the antichrist channels through eloquent speakers to the innocent.

This is how we recognize the antichrist's lies. False teachers are from the world. They speak from the viewpoint of the world. Those people who are worldly listen to them because they appeal to their carnal desires.

People who follow the antichrist's teaching do not recognize the lies because their spirit is squelched, and they do not hear God's voice.

There are no secrets withheld from our Father. God knows everything through the Holy Spirit who lives in us. God's child recognizes Spirit's voice and follows His leadership.

Whenever our heart condemns us, we walk away and set our heart at rest in His presence. If our heart does not condemn us, we have confidence to do what pleases Him.

God's Perfect Love

I John 4:6-21

Our Father's love for us is like the love of a parent who witnesses their child's first breath. God loves us completely before we come to know Him.

This is how God has demonstrated His abiding love for us: He sent His one and only Son into the world that we might live a fulfilled life through him.

We can't earn God's love, for it is an eternal gift. His love takes us from death to life and on to the Kingdom of Heaven and eternal life. And this is God's love: He set aside his Son's life as an atoning sacrifice for our sins before we ever knew Him.

These are ways we know we have God's love in us. Loving God and fearing God do not exist together. Perfect love drives out fear of God from our heart because fear implies punishment. The one who fears God lives without Him and is not made perfect in His love. God's love and hate do not exist together. Perfect love purges hate from our heart because hate signifies bitter hostility exists toward another person. The one who hates lives without God in their life. A person fools themselves if they believe they can live this life with hate in their heart and still come before God with confidence when their time in this world ends.

God's love lacks nothing.

We care for those who touch our life with the love of God that is in us.

Our Father perfects us in His love as He holds onto us in a way no one can take us from His grasp.

His love defines us as a person as we live our life in His love. Just like Jesus, God's love is completed in this world through us.

When we love as God loves us, we can have confidence on the judgement day because in this world we are like Him.

Concluding Remarks

I John 5:1-21

Dear friends, we have shared the same love for many years. When God's word was fresh and His Spirit in us was new, I watched you overcome your world with a zeal for the Lord. You were full of faith and the Holy Spirit, so it was not a burden for you to obey God's commands.

You followed Spirit's voice in your daily life while you loved God with all your heart, soul, and mind, and loved your neighbor as yourself.

Everyone shared what they had with each other and worshipped God in spirit and truth.

We all rejoiced as the churches grew with new believers who were added to your numbers.

I am now concerned some who belonged to us have stepped from the Light to darkness. They have decided to forsake their faith in Jesus Christ to follow the antichrists who live in our midst. Pray for them because we know anyone born of God does not continue to live a worldly lifestyle.

I write to you now so you might believe in the name of the Son of God and be confident you have eternal life.

This is how we know we are God's child: Jesus came to us with a countenance filled with love, mercy and truth, and a Spirit filled with life and light. Whoever claims to be God's child lives as Jesus did in our Father's perfect love.

The Life appeared. I have seen him.

You study Christian history and decide for yourself what you believe. The history you consider now was John's reality. John and Jesus grew up together as children and matured together as young men, then adults.

John witnessed God's spirit descend upon Jesus when he was baptized by John the Baptist. He lived with Jesus for three years as Jesus healed the sick and demon-possessed, and taught the people a new path to salvation. He watched Jesus raise Lazarus from the dead.

John stood at the cross on Skull Mountain and watched Jesus die. Three days later, he met my friend Peter at Jesus' empty tomb. Jesus' body was gone, yet the linen strips and his burial cloth remained. Hours passed, then, Jesus came to John and the other disciples. He revealed his pierced hands, feet, and side.

Jesus was alive! Jesus stayed with John and the other disciples for forty days. He taught them many things about the Kingdom of God as he prepared them to minister in his name with Spirit. When the time came for Jesus to leave, John stood with the other disciples on Mount Olive and watched Jesus ascend to Heaven.

After Jesus departed, John huddled with all the other disciples. They were fearful, yet excited as they waited on the promised Holy Spirit to arrive. When God's Spirit came upon John in Jerusalem on the Day of Pentecost, his life changed forever.

John knew what love was by the way he witnessed Jesus love his Father, the way Jesus loved him, and the way he saw Jesus set aside his life to face a grueling death at the end for an unlovable people.

John trusted God's truth because he listened to Him while Jesus Christ spoke His truth.

He never doubted himself in his circumstance because Jesus always cared for his physical needs when John lived with him.

It was easy for John to believe in the name of Jesus Christ because he saw Jesus and lived with him. John laid his head on Jesus' chest at their last supper.

Blessed are you who have not seen all this and yet you still believe.

CPSIA information can be obtained
at www.ICGtesting.com
Printed in the USA
LVHW080525230721
693276LV00004B/23